# THE LUXURY SHOPPING GUIDE TO LONDON

## Nicholas Courtney

THE VENDOME PRESS

ALSO BY NICHOLAS COURTNEY

*Shopping and Cooking in Europe*
*The Tiger*
*Diana, Princess of Wales*
*Royal Children*
*Prince Andrew*
*Sporting Royals*
*Diana, Princess of Fashion*
*Queen Elizabeth, the Queen Mother*
*The Very Best of British*
*In Society: the Brideshead Years*
*Princess Anne*

Copyright © Nicholas Courtney, 1987

Illustrations by Mark McLaughlin

Published in Great Britain by
George Weidenfeld & Nicolson Limited
91 Clapham High Street
London SW4 7TA

Published in the USA by
The Vendome Press
515 Madison Avenue
New York City 10022

Distributed in the USA by
Rizzoli International Publications
597 Fifth Avenue
New York City 10017

Library of Congress Cataloging-in-Publication Data

Courtney, Nicholas.
    The luxury guide to shopping in London.

    1. Shopping — England — London — Guide-books. 2. London
(England) — Description — 1981 — Guide-books.
I. Title.
TX337.G72L63    1987      380.1'45'00025421      87-14219
ISBN 0-86565-088-8

Printed and bound in Great Britain

# Contents

FOR VANESSA

# Introduction

Shopping in London, particularly luxury shopping, is an undoubted joy. Apart from the quality and availability of everything on offer, the shopping districts are, compared with other capital cities, generally compact. This is because either the same type of shops (like tailors or antique shops) tend to cling together in traditional areas, or the shops selling goods in the same price bracket share the same neighbourhood, although this is partly due to the levels of their rents. Each area, however, does have its own, distinct character.

The heartland of luxury shopping in London is, as it always has been, Mayfair – that maze of streets roughly bounded by Oxford Street to the north, Bond Street to the east, Piccadilly to the south and Park Lane to the west – and its immediate environs, like St James's (below Piccadilly). Of them all, Bond Street and New Bond Street, and the streets leading off them, have the greatest *cachet*, while St James's, that criss-cross of streets between Jermyn Street and Pall Mall, has the more elegant façades. Tucked away even further are the arcades, the Burlington Arcade, Princes Arcade and Royal Opera Arcade.

To the west of Mayfair is Knightsbridge, a more residential area, but with pockets of smart shops. Sloane Street and Knightsbridge form the axis of the shopping area with a few notable streets running parallel to or leading off them such as Brompton Arcade, Beauchamp Place (smart, but just misses being exclusive), Walton Street (smart but hell for parking). Walton Street leads into the Fulham Road (geographically in South Kensington) with a fair share of up-market shops. Here, too, is what is called 'the Brown Mile' where all the antique shops (mostly fine English furniture) have brown shop fronts.

Leading from Sloane Square (at the southern end of Sloane Street), is the King's Road. With a very few exceptions, it is given over to jeans and cheap shoes, trendy boutiques and transitory fashions. Further west still, is Fulham with its share of antique shops and a new, small nucleus of specialized shops.

Moving east from Mayfair is Covent Garden, which can be described as 'up and coming', if it has not arrived. The shops here, particularly within the renovated Covent Garden Market, tend to be rather 'crafty'. Soho, while host to the pornographic trade and one of London's red light districts, has some excellent, specialized food shops, French butchers, fishmongers, Italian delicatessens, and the like.

This guide has been carefully planned for the casual and dedicated shopper alike. Listed alphabetically for easy reference, there is also a comprehensive geographical index followed by a general index which details each individual item. With the overseas visitor in mind, a glossary of English terms and comparative sizes chart have also been included. Everything listed, with a few, notable exceptions, is new. However, with London as one of the antique centres in the world, the antique shops and galleries are a complete subject in themselves – try the *Guide to the Antique Shops of London*, published by the Antique Collectors' Club. In *The Luxury Shopping Guide to London*, there are only passing references to antique shops as they appear geographically.

There are no prices in the book. Even with the low levels of inflation (at least, at the time of writing), prices do have a habit of creeping up, so they have been deliberately omitted. There is a maxim that 'one cannot afford to buy cheap clothes': the majority of these luxury shops are expensive (often there is the name and the location to pay for). But expense is only comparative. Frequently, the more expensive item is the better value, a basic question of economics. A pair of ready-to-wear shoes may cost £80 and last for less than two years; a pair of hand-made shoes may cost £600 and last 30 years – £40 as opposed to £20 per annum respectively.

Most of the shops included take all the major credit cards: Access or Master Card, American Express, Visa or Barclaycard and Diners Club. Those few shops that do not take any cards at all are shown 'No credit cards'.

# Notes to Shopping in London

THE STAFF

Most of the larger, grander shops in the West End employ commissionaires, ex-Servicemen from the Corps of Commissionaires. Many have been there for years and are as much a part of the establishment as the façade. They are invariably well turned out, are helpful, will open doors and find taxis for customers. Larger stores, and some of the boutiques like Chanel, have their own, liveried doormen. Both doorman and commissionaire would not be averse to a small tip for taxi-hailing (only) but, unlike the hotel doormen, would not expect it.

Unlike their counterparts in many of the world's capitals, the staff in London shops are generally polite and courteous. On the whole, they know their jobs, and have been well trained. There is a great sense of continuity too in many of the older shops, where the staff never seem to change.

## SHOPPING

Shopping, particularly luxury shopping, is an especially gentle, unhurried affair. There seems to be all the time in the world (except for Christmas, when there is none). Many shops have chairs and sofas, some will offer their customers a cup of coffee or tea, even a drink. Once the purchase has been made, most shops will generally deliver (in the London area) if asked – it used to be social suicide to be seen carrying a parcel anywhere in the West End.

## BESPOKE *VERSUS* READY-TO-WEAR

Arguments over the merits and demerits of buying ready-to-wear, as opposed to bespoke (*see* Glossary page 163) or couture, have raged for decades; yet the basis for those arguments has now changed. It used to be a question of price, but now many off-the-peg clothes, especially suits, have overtaken the traditional tailors' charges. It was also a question of exclusivity, but now many of the better designers will only produce a limited edition of any one design so it is virtually couture. On the other hand, bespoke clothes and shoes are all hand-made, exclusively for the customer. As such, they should fit exactly and last a lifetime.

## BARGAINING

In most shops, the price shown for new items is the price payable and is not negotiable. However, while it is perhaps not the best idea to treat Bond Street like a souk, there are exceptions. Antique and picture dealers will expect to 'deal' a little, as will most jewelers on the more important pieces. In other shops, a particularly large order might attract a discount (if you do not ask, you certainly will not receive). Overseas visitors can reclaim the V.A.T.

## DUTY FREE SHOPPING

The trouble with most official government schemes is that they turn something that is straightforward and simple to understand into a heinous exercise that is too complicated, and not worth the trouble to unravel. The Value Added Tax Refund pamphlet (V.A.T. Retail Exports [March 1985] Notice 704) is one of those. However, such are the savings (the V.A.T. rate is 15%) and so simple the process of claiming the refund, that it is well worth the effort. With only a few exceptions, every shop covered by the book operates a V.A.T. refund scheme.

Visitors who can reclaim the V.A.T. fall into two categories: Overseas Visitors (those who have not spent more than a full year in the United Kingdom in the two preceding years, and who intend to leave within three months), and European Community Travellers, who live within the European Community (outside the U.K.) and who intend to leave within three months.

The process of reclaiming the V.A.T. is slightly different for the two categories. The Overseas Visitors should produce a passport or some other form of identification to prove to the shop that they are eligible for the refund. The customer is then given a Retail Export Scheme form to be filled in, and a stamped addressed envelope (some shops make a small administration charge). The goods should be shown to the Customs Officer on departure, the form signed and stamped by him, and sent back to the relevant shop in the stamped addressed envelope. The shop will then refund the V.A.T. in the form agreed at the time – either by sterling cheque (often a bore) or, better, as a credit on a credit card. All is not lost if you forget to have the form signed on departure, as it can be done at home by a notary public, or someone similar. Goods shipped direct should be purchased without the V.A.T.

For the European Community Travellers (ECT), the process is slightly different in that there is a minimum value of each item (or group of articles normally sold as a set – like table-cloth, place mats and napkins etc) of £250 (£55 for the Republic of Ireland; £200 for Greece and Denmark). Check that the limit has not risen again since the time of writing. As with the Overseas Visitor, ECTs should then show their passports or identification and fill in the Retail Export Scheme form and collect the addressed envelope (no stamp). On arrival at the home country, the form and the goods should be declared, the local taxes paid and the form signed and stamped by the Customs. The form is then returned to the shop (in the supplied envelope) and the refund is sent – again agree on the method of payment, cheque or credit card, at the time.

Certainly, every shop covered in this book which operates the scheme would be only too happy to advise.


THE SALES

With only a very few exceptions, every London shop has an annual sale, often two sales a year – New Year or just post-Christmas, and summer, anytime after the end of June and early July. Recently, shops selling nothing but designer clothes at sale prices have sprung up. Sales fall into two categories: those which are selling off old stock at reduced prices and those, like the big stores, which bring in a whole new stock of seconds and imperfect goods that are marked down in price. Often, however, it is a combination of the two.

## TRANSPORTING

London shops are particularly good at wrapping up all purchases, often gift wrapped in their own, special paper, at no extra charge. Most will deliver (in the London area if asked nicely) either free, or at a nominal charge: they are quite prepared to send anything by post or special carrier, even ship abroad, at a fee. However, there are specialist shippers for the dedicated shopper, who will collate the purchases and forward them on.

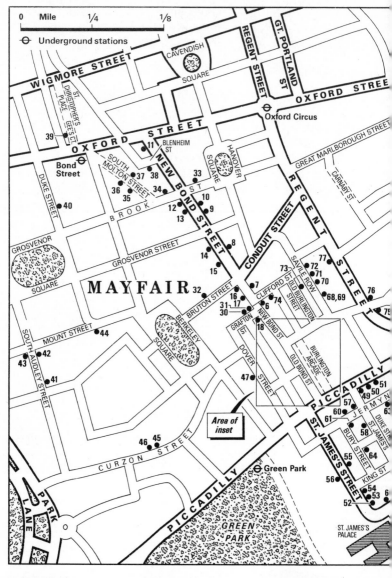

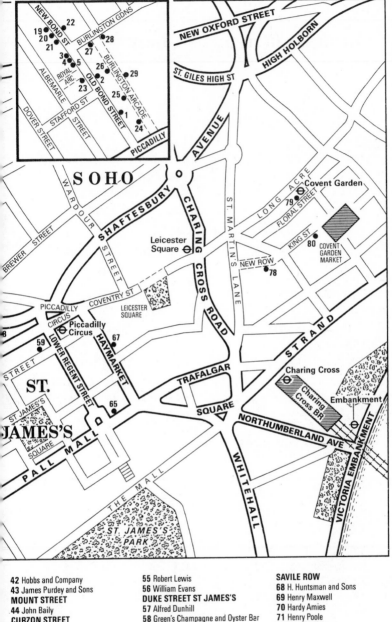

# Comparative Sizes Chart

WOMEN

*Dresses, Blouses, knitwear*

| | | | | | | | |
|---|---|---|---|---|---|---|---|
| UK | 10 | 12 | 14 | 16 | 18 | 20 | 22 |
| Europe | 40 | 42 | 44 | 46 | 48 | 50 | 59 |
| USA | 8 | 10 | 12 | 14 | 16 | 18 | 20 |

*Shoes*

| | | | | | | | |
|---|---|---|---|---|---|---|---|
| UK | 3 | $3\frac{1}{2}$ | 4 | $4\frac{1}{2}$ | 5 | $5\frac{1}{2}$ | 6 |
| Europe | $35\frac{1}{2}$ | 36 | 37 | $37\frac{1}{2}$ | 38 | 39 | $39\frac{1}{2}$ |
| USA | 4 | $4\frac{1}{2}$ | 5 | $5\frac{1}{2}$ | 6 | $6\frac{1}{2}$ | 7 |

MEN

*shirts*

| | | | | | | | |
|---|---|---|---|---|---|---|---|
| UK | $14\frac{1}{2}$ | 15 | $15\frac{1}{2}$ | 16 | $16\frac{1}{2}$ | 17 | $17\frac{1}{2}$ |
| Europe | 37 | 38 | 39 | 40 | 41 | 42 | 43 |
| USA | $14\frac{1}{2}$ | 15 | $15\frac{1}{2}$ | 16 | $16\frac{1}{2}$ | 17 | $17\frac{1}{2}$ |

*trousers*

| | | | | | | | |
|---|---|---|---|---|---|---|---|
| UK | 28 | 30 | 32 | 34 | 36 | 38 | 40 |
| Europe | 71 | 76 | 81 | 85 | 91 | 97 | 102 |
| USA | 28 | 30 | 32 | 34 | 36 | 38 | 40 |

*shoes*

| | | | | | | | |
|---|---|---|---|---|---|---|---|
| UK | 7 | $7\frac{1}{2}$ | 8 | $8\frac{1}{2}$ | 9 | $9\frac{1}{2}$ | 10 |
| Europe | $40\frac{1}{2}$ | 41 | 42 | $42\frac{1}{2}$ | 43 | $43\frac{1}{2}$ | $44\frac{1}{2}$ |
| USA | 8 | $8\frac{1}{2}$ | 9 | $9\frac{1}{2}$ | 10 | $10\frac{1}{2}$ | 11 |

# J. A. Allen

■ 1 LOWER GROSVENOR PLACE            828 8855 or 834 5606
BUCKINGHAM PALACE ROAD
SW1W 0EL
(*Horse books*)

When it comes to books about horses, there is no greater authority than Joe Allen, founder and sole-owner of J. A. Allen and Co Ltd, booksellers and publishers since 1926. There are no frills in his shop (aptly sited opposite the Crown Equerry's Grace and Favour house in the Royal Mews), just thousands of volumes from floor to ceiling on every conceivable aspect of the horse. So complete is his stock, that if he finds some equine subject that has not been covered, or adequately covered, Joe Allen puts on his publisher's hat and commissions the work himself.

The staff who work there have been chosen for their specialized knowledge of horses and riding rather than any deep understanding of literature and books. Thus, given even the gist of what the customer is looking for, any of them will be able to recommend a suitable title. J. A. Allen also produce quarterly catalogues of books on racing, hunting and equitation, from which their customers may order books by post.

Above the comparative order of the shop is a maze of rooms where the equine antiquarian and out-of-print books are shelved, all for sale. Joe Allen also offers a unique service of being able to track down practically any equestrian book, from a sixteenth-century Italian work on equitation to a modern classic. Having dealt with millions of books throughout his life, it would have to be a very obscure title indeed that he cannot 'visualize' and know where to lay his hands on a copy.

Joe Allen is a jovial man, bubbling over with an infectious enthusiasm for life and his books. The only concession to his age (he admits to being nearer 80 than 70) is not to go into the shop on Mondays. Instead, he is there, single handed, on Saturdays which gives him the chance to keep in touch with his customers.

OPEN    Monday to Friday 9.30 am to 5.30 pm, Saturday 10.00 am to 1.00 pm

# Aquascutum

■ 100 REGENT STREET            734 6090
W1A 2AQ
(*Rainwear and traditional clothes*)

The shield that the Royal College of Arms designed for Aquascutum for their Grant of Arms has a white band across the top (representing a rain cloud), and blue with white droplets below (symbolizing rain). Over this veritable weathershield is a crown representing excellence, and under it, their motto *In Hoc Scuto Fidemus* (We have faith in this shield). Their customers have also put their faith in that shield, or *aqua scutum*, since their founding in 1851.

Aquascutum's reputation was based on the original idea of showerproofing woollen cloth, and tailoring this material into well-cut coats. These weatherproof coats instantly became fashionable, and, of course, were hugely practical. During the First World War, the standard issue of officers' cotton coats was useless, so for the discerning (and the well-off) Aquascutum produced a heavy-duty, wool gabardine coat with an oil-dressed lining to combat the cold, the wet and the mud of the trenches. The basic design of high collar, sleeve straps, epaulettes, deep yoke back and D rings on the belt was purely functional. However, after the war, these coats remained popular, in Great Britain, in Europe and in the United States – it became almost obligatory wear for screen detectives, from Philip Marlowe (Humphrey Bogart and Robert Mitchum) to Inspector Clouseau (Peter Sellers). For years, Aquascutum catered solely for men, but shortly after the First World War they made for women also.

Today, that traditional trenchcoat with those features is still made, now in a slightly lighter material than the original. There are also a seemingly limitless number of adaptations of that original coat, with differing fabric weights, colours and sizes, including size 4 *petite* for the Japanese. Although the basic idea remains constant, the styles change marginally from year to year to follow fashion trends. There is also a wide variety of linings, like their own distinctive Club Check in navy, camel and beige, and silk, even with a detachable wool lining, which, when introduced, doubled as a dressing gown.

Besides these famous weathercoats, Aquascutum are renowned for their other clothes. They claim that 'style is never out of fashion' and they have their own factories which guarantees quality.

On the ground floor, there is everything by way of men's clothes, save for suits and coats. Here, there are banks of shirts and sweaters, shelves of their own men's toiletries, racks of trousers and a speciality, a selection of blousons, in fact everything that could possibly be needed all on one floor – if your luggage was lost at the airport, you could replace everything here, including the luggage. Their display is inviting: a dining table covered with shirts, a circular table laid out with ties like the blades of a polychrome fan of a jet engine.

The first floor is also given over to men (and ladies' rainwear), with suits of every description and a splendid range of town and country coats and rainwear – their covert coat looks special. The second floor is given over entirely to women. Their clothes could not be described as high fashion, although they do bend with the current trend. Thus, these clothes are thoroughly wearable and timeless. Aquascutum go in for 'suggestion' selling – like placing a rack of blazers over a rack of co-ordinating skirts, with a row of blouses nearby. It is all very subtle and tastefully done. The staff are highly trained and courteous, and will give an opinion, if asked.

Throughout the whole shop, there is plenty of choice with colour (five shades of pink for a cashmere scarf should be enough for anyone), style and sizing, as they carry a large stock. This shop is thoroughly traditional and English, wherein lies its greatest strength.

OPEN    Monday to Saturday 9.30 am to 5.30 pm (Thursday until

7.00 pm)

# Asprey

■ 165–169 NEW BOND STREET                     493 6767
W1Y 0AR
(*Jewelry and leatherwork, particularly luggage, presents*)

It would be difficult not to eulogize over Asprey's, for it is one of the most fascinating and luxurious shops in the world. Apart from their clients (the word customer does not seem quite right here), Asprey's are only interested in quality, and the service that goes with quality. The shop opened in the late eighteenth century, quite modestly, but with those founding Aspreys' insistence on perfection, they had to move more and more up-market with their goods to keep pace with their high standards. It was not long before they moved to their present address in Bond Street, where they were renowned for their 'articles of exclusive design and high quality, whether for personal adornment or

personal accomplishment', and with a reputation 'to endow with richness and beauty the tables and homes of people of refinement and discernment'. A just claim then, as indeed it is true today.

Asprey's appeals at every level. Their clients are as diverse in their taste, as they are in their pockets. Good taste should never, indeed cannot, be defined. What may appear vulgar to some is perfection to another; what would look monstrous in an English country house, is absolutely right in a marble hall in the Middle East. Asprey's know their clients' needs exactly, and make certain that they can fulfil them. Whatever it is, a piece of jewelry, an *objet d'art*, something worked in a precious metal or in leather, antique or modern, it will all bear that unmistakable Asprey mark of quality and workmanship.

Few who enter through those double, bow-fronted doors that slide open as though one door, could possibly describe the decor, other than that the carpet is green and the lighting is bright and welcoming. The eye is drawn instantly to that rich, and varied feast of Asprey's goods throughout the shop.

There are rows of mahogany and glass cabinets around the outside and down the centre of the main hall, each with its own particular theme. Here are those little 9- and 18-carat gold or solid silver 'trinkets', the cigar cutter or swizzle-stick, the cuff-

12

links (even sets of dress-studs set with rubies and diamonds), the key-rings and the money clips (with a cabochon sapphire), each small enough to slip into a Christmas cracker. Here too are the watches. Asprey's have a splendid collection, including many of their own make with beautiful bracelets and straps. There is also the best of the rest, such as Coran, Rolex and Piaget (downstairs is the watch-repair service). They are also renowned for their own clocks, both antique and modern, especially their carriage clocks and quartz travelling clocks in pretty frames. Asprey's do not have to show the provenance of anything they sell by dressing it up in their colours of purple and green, the only exceptions being a pen, a lighter, and bridge cards . . . and their race horse.

One of the many strengths of Asprey's is that the majority of their goods, be it jewelry, gold, silver or leather, is made by their own craftsmen, in their own workshops, very often to their own designs. Nothing is extraordinary to them. If they do not have it, then it can be made, although most of the silverwork is pretty standard, like the Adam-style candle sticks, tea and coffee services, salvers and bowls and, of course, the table decorations of pheasants and partridges. Exact scale replicas in silver of every kind of aircraft, boat, train, and tank is a constant Asprey challenge. So, too, is the positive menagerie of the more exotic wild animals: lions and tigers, cheetahs and leopards, elephants and gorillas cast in silver gilt and inlaid with precious stones, or exquisitely carved from such semi-precious stones as rock-crystal, malachite, and amethyst. Finely carved birds of prey hover over crystal; kingfishers sit above an agate water with golden lilies. Here there are exquisite *objets d'art* of crystal and gold, enamel and precious stones whose design, originality, and workmanship are equal to anything produced by Fabergé (they sell his work too, upstairs). The same is true of their jewelry, all beautifully displayed in a room within a room, used for both their modern and antique pieces.

Although they did not win a prize for their dressing case when they entered it at the Great Exhibition in 1851, Asprey's at least earned an 'honourable mention'. They are still making ladies' dressing cases, and everything to go in them (some are old and have been completely remade). They also make everything for men in the same line (what they coyly term 'Gentlemen's Wet Packs') complete with silver- or ivory-backed hair brushes, silver razors and shaving brushes. Asprey's have always been the last word in luggage – there are fine crocodile cases and many other leathers, like pig-skin and calf. A new range is in French tapestry with black leather trim; a traditional range incorporates cases in green canvas with pigskin trim. Again, everything in leather can be made to order, from a wallet to a cabin trunk. There is nothing more elegant than an Asprey's handbag in crocodile or lizard (and other leathers and fabrics), nor is there anything much smarter than their attaché-case in bridle-hide, or again crocodile. Their leather-bound photograph albums are legion, as are their bound books (Asprey's have taken over the famous book-binder, Sangorski and Sutcliffe).

For *al fresco* dining, there are picnic baskets (and rugs) of all sizes, from a twosome to something the size of an old-fashioned laundry basket for a banquet for 12. For dining inside there is the table-top room (upstairs) with everything for the table-top by way of silver and glass (other ceramics, with such treats as Herend dinner services and ornaments, are below).

It seems almost a pity to disturb anything upstairs in Asprey's two antique rooms by buying something, as all the furniture seems to go so well together. But here they deal mostly in Georgian furniture (although they do stretch their dates from 1680 to 1820). There is always a fine selection of dining tables and sets of dining chairs, side tables and gaming tables, long-case clocks and looking-glasses and much more. Next door are the smaller items, decanters and old glass, the aforementioned Fabergé pieces and eighteenth-century gold boxes, not forgetting another Asprey speciality, turned-ivory chess sets.

At Asprey's, everyone is treated as an important client; seriously important clients are treated to a special room to view, or a viewing after shop hours, while the really serious clients are treated to a private visit by the Chairman, John Asprey (the staff say that his demands are far greater than any client's, and it shows). Asprey's is an experience in shopping and exciting present-buying. The sight of that tell-tale, purple, gift wrapping (or the white Christmas cracker) on a present can only quicken the pulse: open it, and you have the ultimate.

OPEN Monday to Friday 9.00 am to 5.30 pm, Saturday 9.00 am to 1.00 pm

# John Baily and Sons

■ 116 MOUNT STREET, W1 499 1833
(*Poulterers, game dealers and butchers*)

The strength of John Baily and Sons, established in 1720, is that they are prime, traditional butchers, poulterers and game dealers. They are traditional in that everything is fresh (perish the thought of anything frozen); prime as everything is specially prepared for the customer.

Here are the best in meat: Scottish beef, Danish veal, English lamb and pork, butchered in either English or French cuts. They also dress their meat to order, with such cuts as saddles of lamb and French trimmed lamb cutlets. For 'dinner party fare', they have specially prepared cuts, like crown roasts, stuffed baby kid, beef olives, stuffed loin of pork or veal, the stuffing being prepared in their own kitchens.

As traditional butchers, Baily's chickens are all fresh and sold with their 'insides', head and feet (they are, of course, cleaned and gutted for the customer, on the spot). Chickens can be prepared in many ways, boned, boned and stuffed, or in 'oven ready' dishes like chicken Kiev. Baily's have always had a reputation of being one of the best game dealers in London. Here there is every kind of game in season, including a ready supply of hare, squabs, even guinea fowl. It arrives 'in the feather', is plucked and dressed with a piece of *lardo*, Italian pork fat. Venison is sold only as a haunch or a saddle, and can be boned and rolled to order.

No butcher is complete without a sausage machine. Baily's sausages are predictably superior with such treats as English breakfast, venison and game, as well as their own recipe for spiced veal, pork and beef.

OPEN   Monday to Friday 7.00 am to 4.00 pm, Saturday 7.00 am to 1.00 pm
No credit cards

# Basile

■ 21 NEW BOND STREET                              493 3618
W1
(*Italian boutique*)

This is a bright and colourful shop, with bright and colourful women's clothes, (unlike nature, the men's clothes are more sombre). What is more, the staff are bright and colourful too.

Here, there is a whole range of designer women's clothes, for both day and evening wear. Each collection is carefully put together; blouses coordinate with skirts, that go with jackets, which in turn go with everything else. They are also renowned for their coats, invariably striking in cut and colour. Their tailoring, from their own workrooms in Milan, is the best, as is the choice of natural fabrics they use for all their clothes. There is a seamstress on the premises who will alter any of their clothes.

At Basile, there is always something new and exciting, even exotic, especially for evening. The house style is either very tight fitting or loose and flowing, quite often in black. Typical is their tight, black, ruched-silk skirt or the flowing black chiffon skirt and top, embroidered with marquisette in moons and stars. Their accessories, like their polychrome selection of tights and stockings, have all been chosen with their clothes in mind.

Downstairs is Basile's men's department. Their clothes are more conventional than of late, with muted colours and greys. Their suits and coats are classic and Italian; their leather jackets finely made. Among this full range of clothes, of suits and coats, of jackets and pure wool trousers, is a splendid selection of Paisley socks. Luggage, by way of a large bag and a strong, leather suitcase, is a new innovation.

Service is very personal here: the staff know their regular customers, just as the regular customers know them. The ultimate must be when one of the staff telephones to say, 'We have just the thing for you'.

OPEN   Monday to Saturday 10.00 am to 6.00 pm

# ■ The Beauchamp Place Shop

■  55 BEAUCHAMP PLACE                                    589 4118/4155
   SW3
   (*Good, British women's designer fashions*)

This is a shop for the type of woman who is never in London for the weekend. The Beauchamp Place Shop represents just a few of the top British and European designers – the likes of Marion Foale, Sheilagh Brown and Edina Ronay of the former; Ventilo, Emmanuelle Khanh and Cerruti of the latter. Despite their differing provenance, the end result is not dissimilar as all have that same English classic look, one that suits an English way of life. Their clothes are mostly day wear and, therefore, definitely 'non-glitzy'. The collections are all carefully chosen in that just as each individual designer's collection is totally co-ordinated, so are all the other designers' collections compatible one with another.

The shop is smart and bright, with smart, bright, designer-clad assistants. Just to help that woman who is never in London at the weekend on her way to the country, The Beauchamp Place Shop have a fine range of J. and M. Davidson soft-leather luggage.

OPEN   Monday to Friday 10.00 am to 6.00 pm (Wednesday until 6.30 pm), Saturday 11.00 am to 6.00 pm

# Beaudesert

■ 8 SYMONS STREET                                    730 5102
  SW3
  (*Four-poster bed manufacturers*)

The new owners of this shop, being unhappy with the original name, *The Bed Chamber*, cast around for something that conjured up a picture of Georgian proportion, Regency elegance and traditional craftsmanship. Berkley Paget and Gabrielle Langer lit upon *Beaudesert* – those clever students of genealogy would recognize the name as that of the Staffordshire seat of the Pagets; while those well versed in portraiture would more easily recognize their logo, the one-legged Henry Paget, Earl of Uxbridge of Plas Newydd in Anglesey.

Whatever the origins of the nomenclature of the shop, this is *the* place to find the ultimate in new four-poster beds. Beaudesert have their own workshops in Northumberland where their craftsmen make up the complete bed with any one of the standard range of posts. Each post is an exact copy of the eighteenth- and nineteenth-century original. Some are carved mahogany, like the Wheatleaf, Halton, Regency, Hepplewhite and the plainer Standard, while two, Hexam and Green, are just painted. Occasionally they stock antique bed-posts which can then be made up to order. Having their own workshop means that they can also build any bed on request. They have endless ideas, illustrations and books of every conceivable bed to choose from, and are confident that they can make anything for a client from a sketch or photograph (they have yet to copy the famous state beds from Erdigg or Houghton, but the time may come).

Beaudesert do have their own standard range of hangings, mostly chintzes, which are obviously chosen with that purpose in mind. These chintzes are exclusive to them, being taken from the Archives of Warner and G. P. Baker who also control the printing. They are always in stock so, unlike many fabric shops who have to order their material, there is no delay. However, as a large and imposing bed is the major item of a bedroom, the hangings more often are chosen with the client's decoration in mind rather than the other way round. Where Berkley Paget is technical and knows about constructing beds, Gabrielle Langer is an interior decorator. It is not uncommon for a client to come in to discuss the hangings for a bed and end up with a scheme for the whole bedroom, sometimes the whole house.

Besides these beds, there are other pieces of fine, reproduction furniture, a Louis XVI sofa copied from the original in the Villa d'Este, a bed-end stool and various French *fauteuils*. The Beaudesert sofa and armchairs are large, English and much more comfortable than the French furniture. Beaudesert are also noted for their lamps and cushions, some frilly, others worked in tapestry.

The shop has a solid, English feel about it tempered with good taste (as far as that can be defined). Both partners are genial and generally there (usually downstairs surrounded by swatches of material and drawings of inviting beds). There is always an up-to-date catalogue with price list sent on request.

OPEN   Monday to Friday 9.30 am to 5.30 pm

# Bellville Sassoon

■ 73 PAVILION ROAD                                      235 3087/5801
SW1
(*Fashion house*)

Two 'stone' Imperial eagles guard the front of Bellville Sassoon's shop in Pavilion Road, a long, cobbled mews that runs parallel to Sloane Street. Inside, the shop is plain and functional, the decoration coming from the bright and colourful dresses themselves (at least when bright and cheerful colours are in fashion).

The company and its name remained intact after Belinda Bellville retired, as did the designing and that inimitable Bellville Sassoon style which have all been carried on by David Sassoon. That style is romantic, especially with their famous evening dresses. As with all their clothes, both day and evening, they have managed to combine an elegance with sophistication, yet at the same time retaining a fresh and exciting, youthful, look. The choice of fabric naturally changes with the seasons, as do the colours that follow the current fashion.

Like the other top fashion houses, Bellville Sassoon has two ready-to-wear collections a year, shown with the London Designer Collections, and sold in their shop and elsewhere. In addition, they have two annual collections for their couture clients (either very grand and international or conventional 'gentlewomen') in their shop. It takes at least a month with three fiittings for anyting couture.

Another house speciality is wedding dresses ('if prepared to pay and wait long enough'), and the dress for the MOB (the mother of the bride).

Should you watch the television news of some Royal occasion, or the arrival of some major film star, or just attend some

18

society wedding, the chances are that the protagonist is dressed by Bellville Sassoon.

OPEN    Monday to Friday 9.30 am to 5.30 pm

## Berry Bros and Rudd

■ 3 ST JAMES'S STREET                          930 1888/5331
SW1A 1EG                                   *Export* 930 5631
(*Wine merchant*)

Berry Bros and Rudd, established in the 1690s, may not be the oldest wine merchants in London, but they have occupied Number Three, St James's Street since 1731, which certainly

19

makes them the oldest wine merchant in the same premises. The continuity goes even further in that it is still a family firm, with a seventh-generation Berry as managing director and a second-generation Rudd as chairman.

Little appears to have changed over the centuries. There is the same, bottle-green, Georgian shop front with the 'Sign of the Coffee Mill' (a reference to their seventeenth-century origins as grocers) swinging above the door. Inside, the rooms are oak-panelled, with wide, elm floor-boards. Engravings of past, famous customers line the walls; ancient bottles fill glass-fronted cabinets. Dominating the room is a huge pair of scales, originally for weighing sacks of coffee, tea and spices, but, from 1765 until comparatively recently, they have weighed their customers. There are nine volumes, filled with some 20,000 names, each with their weight and date recorded (the previous Aga Khan came in to be weighed several times a week when in London). The lists are fascinating, with entries like Beau Brummel, William Pitt, Charles James Fox, Lord Byron, Napoleon III, Rosa Lewis of the Cavendish fame, and Anthony Eden.

With such a venerable history, a period house in a smart street, Berry Bros and Rudd could easily be mistaken for an exclusive, unapproachable, wine merchant. Although they still have grand clients and a particularly senior wine list, they are adamant that they are a general wine merchant that serves every palate and pocket. Berry Bros are strong on French wines, particularly claret (they are the only wine merchants to maintain an office in Bordeaux). Their list is no less exacting for their vintage champagnes, burgundies, chablis, Loire wines and some hocks. Many of these fine wines also come in both half bottles and magnums.

Alongside these fine vintages are the everyday drinking wines. Berry Bros have acceptable red and white house wines, and their own very drinkable 'Good Ordinary Claret', and champagne. There is also a fine range of carefully selected, French country wines for everyday drinking, together with other wines from Italy, Spain (Rioja), Portugal, Australia, Hungary and England. Many of these wines can be tried in a mixed case, or in their tasting room upstairs.

Berry Bros and Rudd are also good on their fortified wines, especially vintage port and sherry, spirits (they own Cutty Sark Scotch Whisky, distinguished by its natural pale colour), and liqueurs (the King's Ginger Liqueur, made for Edward VII on his doctor's orders, is particularly warming).

The service offered by Berry Bros and Rudd is second to none. The staff are, without exception, all knowledgeable and only too pleased to help and advise. The 20,000-plus customers on the firm's mailing list all receive *Number Three*, a readable, bi-annual magazine giving Berry's news and views on wines, and six or more other mailings a year with details of special offers. Customers' wines (ex-Berry Bros) can be stored at their warehouse in Basingstoke. They prefer to sell wine for drinking rather than investment, although many of their clients are clever (or lucky) enough to finance their drinking of fine wines by buying more than they need, and selling some at auction at Christie's to pay for the next vintage. They give case discounts, 3% up to five cases, 5% up to ten cases and 7% thereafter, and free delivery (on cases) in the United Kingdom.

Although you may not join Berry Bros and Rudd's illustrious clients in their weights' books, they will certainly welcome you to the ranks of their past and present patrons as a client.

OPEN   Monday to Friday 9.30 am to 5.00 pm, closed on Saturday except in December when open 9.30 am to 1.00 pm

# Birger Christensen

■ 170 NEW BOND STREET                                   629 2211
W1Y 9PB
(*Furrier*)

The popularity of the fur-studded soap operas 'Dynasty' and 'Dallas' has not affected the sales of fur coats (the people who buy furs are not affected by such trivia) but they have, apparently, affected their style. Birger Christensen, now incorporating the old established firm of Maxwell Croft, offers innumerable furs and styles each year. Not only are there the 'in house' styles, created by their own designers for the London market, but also collections from Bruce Oldfield (see page 124). Also in their London shop are the collections made by Claude Montana of Paris and by Ralph Lauren (see page 131) of New York.

With so many styles, furs and sizes to choose from, it is possible to find exactly the right coat ready-to-wear. The ground floor is devoted to the boutique where they sell all their fur-lined coats, 'fun-furs' (like their shaggy, dyed-green Tibetan lamb, or red and blue musquash coats), and fur hats of every description. On the first floor there are the exclusive furs – the minks and the sables, the lynx cats and the fox furs. There is also a selection of fur coats for men in beaver, spitz, wolf, even mink.

For those who prefer a bespoke fur coat, Birger Christensen will make it up on the premises. Their own reliable workforce being under the same roof as the shop means that they can guarantee the quality and delivery time of each coat. Despite the

21

steep stairs, the workrooms at the top of the house are well worth the visit. The client is first measured and the style agreed. Then the pelts to be used are chosen from a selection of bundles (generally, the darker the fur, the more expensive the pelt). The first fitting is a linen replica of the coat to check the size and style, then there could be a further two or three fittings for the coat itself before the final fitting (without the lining). When both customer and furrier are totally satisfied, the coat is lined with pure silk and the client's initials are embroidered inside. Depending on the time of year, the whole operation takes between five and six weeks.

Although Birger Christensen do make their own fur-lined rain coats, they will line their clients' own coats, like a Burberry (see page 24). These should be one size larger than normal to take the rabbit or nutria lining.

The eldest son of the chairman, Jens Christensen, is now based in the London shop. He is fifth generation in the family firm, with the experience, together with Maxwell Croft, to buy the best pelts to produce their fine range of coats. The shop itself is smart and modern on the ground floor, but the first floor has a certain faded elegance for the superior and exclusive furs.

OPEN    Monday to Friday 9.30 am to 5.30 pm, Saturday 10.00 am to 5.30 pm
No credit cards

# Browns

■ 23–27 SOUTH MOLTON STREET        491 7833
W1
(*The cream of an international fashion emporium*)

■ 6c SLOANE STREET        493 4232
SW1

There is not much in the marketing field that has not been tried before, especially with clothes, but Browns can honestly claim to be the first to create a 'designer emporium'. Here, numerous different designers' clothes are collected under one roof (in fact five roofs), and, though their works are all totally individual, the end result is a shop selling carefully coordinated clothes.

To achieve this, Browns has a highly organized buying team who operate under the experienced eye of Joan Burstein, owner of the shop (they buy twice-yearly in London, Paris, Milan, New York and Tokyo). The collections they choose are then ruthlessly edited to give that overall, homogeneous and coordinated look.

They are also well tuned to the needs of their customers, and are totally aware of what is happening in the fashion world, from the established designers to those with talent fresh from college. In fact, many of the top designer shops owe their London origins to Browns, for example, Calvin Klein, Giorgio Armani (see page 67) and Ralph Lauren (*see* page 131)).

Browns is made up of five interconnecting shops. The men's shop is at No. 23. Here the same principle of editing collections applies to the whole range of men's clothes, including suits, by designers such as Cerruti, Jasper Conran (*see* page 104), Claude Montana and Go Silk (there is also a fine line of Paisley ties by Etro). Next door, No. 24, is mainly given over to the designs of Azzedine Alaia, with Italy's Romeo Gigli on the lower level. No. 25 houses Sonia Rykiel's collections, and No. 26 is shared by Comme des Garçons, Donna Karan, Missoni and Jil Sander, noted for her classic tailored suits for the working woman. There

is a host of designers at No. 27 that includes Marion Foale, Jean Paul Gautlier, Jean Muir, Rifat Ozbek, and Byblos (the last two being English designers who defected to Milan). The shop in Sloane Street (at No. 6c), is just a smaller version of the South Molton Street shops, but without menswear.

Much is left to the colour and texture of the clothes to give each shop its own, individual decor. The staff (all wearing one of the designers' clothes) are knowledgeable and well trained (they are instructed in each collection, wherever they work, and are shown the possibilities of each garment and how it should be worn). Someone, somewhere in the shop, is bi-lingual in English and a main language.

The strength (and success) of Browns lies in the fact that nothing in their shop is there by chance – what is more, a great deal of effort has gone into putting it there.

OPEN    Monday to Saturday 10.00 am to 6.00 pm (Thursday until 7.00 pm South Molton Street; Wednesday until 7.00 pm Sloane Street)

# Burberrys

■  18 HAYMARKET                                          930 3343
    SW1Y 4DQ
    (*Rainwear specialists*)

■  165 REGENT STREET                                     734 4060
    W1R 8AS

The name Burberry is synonymous with rainwear, as it has been since the original Mr Burberry invented his waterproof material, gabardine, in the late nineteenth century (his was the first waterproof material that was untearable, weatherproof, yet, being a proofed cotton, was cool and comfortable to wear). Since then, Burberry raincoats have been worn everywhere: in the South African War, and the First World War where the first 'Trench Coat' was developed (Lord Kitchener swore by his Burberry, died in it too). They were required wearing in the early days of motoring and for the pioneers in the air such as the popular aviator C. Graham White and Alcock (why not Brown too?). No polar expedition was complete without Burberry's gabardine; Nansen, Scott, Shackleton and Amundsen all swore by theirs. Burberry had, and still does have, Royal approval; Edward VII continually referred to his gabardine cape as his 'Burberry', and the name has stuck for all their rainwear.

Today, the 'Burberry' is equally to be relied upon, both for style (an extension of the original) and practicality, for men and women alike. The trenchcoat lives on in the 'Trench 57', still with its original deep yoke, epaulettes, buckled cuff straps, storm pockets and button-down flaps with the 'D' rings on the belt. The 'Trench 21' is a scaled-down version, while the 'Boston' is similar, only single-breasted. Simplest of all is the 'Piccadilly', single-breasted and smart, like the women's version, called 'The Ladies Walking Burberry'. Women also have three versions of the classic trenchcoat. There is a black evening Burberry in pure silk. Women's coats come in four sizes: petite, long, extra long and extra long +, while the men's are short, regular, long and extra long. There are endless combinations and styles of linings, for both men and women. Most linings are in the distinctive Burberry check, but others are plain in camel, loden cloth, even fur (nutria) and the like. Burberry's will sew them into their coats (if necessary), and also embroider initials. Although the basic style remains the same, the cut changes marginally in line with fashion. With every Burberry comes free insurance against loss (non-renewable) for six months, and a voucher for their valeting service (there is a full valeting service in the basement, but only for their own clothes).

As well-known as the Burberry raincoat is the Burberry check of red, black, grey, white on a fawn background; (they did introduce the 'New Navy check' with a navy background to replace it twenty-five years ago, but still the original remained the favourite). The whole of the Burberry range incorporates these two checks and, with these basic colours, everything else, especially with the women's clothes, is designed to coordinate with them. For example, they do a chic blazer in fawn that is exactly right with the Burberry check skirt and their red shirt; the same works with the blue 'New Navy check' skirt with, say, a red blouson and a cream shirt. They are also branching out, daringly for them, into brighter colours, but still keeping the traditional styles. As with the coats, the styles in all the basic ladies' range remain constant, only the cut alters as fashion dictates. Children's clothes are just clones of the adults.

On the ground floor there is everything for the man. Here, safety and tradition are the overriding influences, nothing very exciting, but all eminently wearable. The blazers (with Burberry buttons), the tweed jackets, the overcoats and the trousers are all nicely made in a wide choice of fabric: the wools and the cashmeres, camel hair and loden (this is a thoroughly British company, and everything is made in their own factories).

Away from this rather staid image, Burberry have a comprehensive 'Active Sports Collection'. Here there is everything for the golfer, from bags and clubs to shoes and the fullest range of golfing clothes (fairweather and foul). Tennis players too can find everything for the court, and off-court, including racket covers and their own tennis balls. There are also some bright sports shirts, emblazoned with the Burberry logo or their name. Their sweaters are brighter too, either plain, cable, Argyle or more daring stripes.

The Burberry check is everywhere (even the cash tills are swathed in it). There is a complete range of luggage, from a brief-case to a cabin trunk. Their cashmere scarves are famous, including one in yellow check that Rupert Bear would be proud of. There is a Burberry fragrance and a Burberry umbrella –even green wellies lined with Burberry check.

Not in the tradition of the teetotal founder, there is a Burberry whisky. Apart from that novelty, everything else continues in the same, fine, Edwardian style. The shop is open and inviting, the staff are there to help, not to chat. The doorman greets customers on arrival and, in wet weather, escorts them on their departure to a taxi under a large, black umbrella (strangely not made by Burberry). At least Trinculo (in *The Tempest*) knew better when he cried: 'Alas, the storm is come again! My best way is to creep under his [Caliban's] gabardine.'

OPEN   Monday to Saturday 9.00 am to 5.30 pm (Thursday until 7.00 pm)

# Butler and Wilson

■ 20 SOUTH MOLTON-STREET          409 2955
  W1
  (*Costume jewelry*)

■ 189 FULHAM ROAD                 352 3045
  SW3

Not that long ago, costume jewelry was used for the stage, or for those who could not afford the real thing. Today, it is an entity in its own right (it has been renamed 'fashion jewelry'). However, whatever the nomenclature, it is invariably novel, fun and exciting, the very reason for wearing it in the first place.

At Butler and Wilson, new, fun and exciting pieces are changing all the time, as everything is designed by the owners, Simon Wilson and Nicky Butler, and made in their own workshops. Here, there is every combination of jewelry, neck-laces of every description, earrings and bracelets, brooches and pins, and just a few rings. There is something for everybody, from the demure Chanel look to the outlandish, with plenty in between. Typical of the Butler and Wilson style is their range of

26

pins: in the shape of lizards, and suns, moons and stars, and flowers. All brilliant and sparkling, fun and wearable.

The pieces are all well-made with paste (a vitreous compound used for artificial gems, not short for pastiche), set in silver, silver gilt or silver and base metal. One range is called 'old elements', which is made up from prewar pieces of jet, marcasite, bakelite, enamel and the like, set in silver and base metal. They also sell a few older pieces of jewelry, mostly art deco (there is a wider selection at the Fulham Road shop) and the odd silver or tortoiseshell picture frame.

Both shops are similar in decor and feel – black with maple-veneer fittings. The concealed lighting is especially good as it picks up the sparkle of the jewelry (and of the staff who care about what they sell). The Butler and Wilson boxes are smart and act as gift wrapping. They will repair any of their own jewelry. So good are their pieces that they can be slipped in with the real thing and no one will notice – or will they?

OPEN   South Molton Street – Monday to Saturday 10.00 am to 6.00 pm (Thursday until 7.00 pm); Fulham Road – Monday to Saturday 10.00 am to 6.00 pm

# Caroline Charles

■ 11 BEAUCHAMP PLACE                      589 5850
SW3
(*Women's designer fashions*)

It is easy to enthuse about Caroline Charles in Beauchamp Place, for here is one of the most inviting places to shop in London. It is bright and open (to the back is a skylight to show off the colours as they really are, as opposed to the tungsten-bulb version of a department store). The decor is soft, greys and pinks, and there are always fresh flowers about the place. It is a friendly shop, with coffee or a glass of wine on offer. It is patently obvious that the staff enjoy working there too; they are welcoming, enthusiastic, and, if asked, ready with advice. What is more, Caroline Charles's designer clothes are pretty special too.

There is a definite Caroline Charles 'look', which, for those who know, is instantly recognizable. Her clothes are basically traditional, but are set apart by the design, the cut and the choice (and quality) of the fabric (Paisley prints are a particular hall-mark of her clothes). They are made above the shop in her own workrooms; she can also alter for a nominal charge. Here, everything co-ordinates with everything else, not just in that particular range or collection, but also with past (and future) collections. So for example, with a Caroline Charles tailored lightweight wool suit, there are the blouses, the sweaters, the scarves and the belts, not to mention the coat and the odd piece of jewelry to go with it. Furthermore, as her clothes are so well cut they will last for several seasons, and can be added to continually. They also suit all ages and shapes. Many of her customers will shop nowhere else, for here they can find all they need, and be certain of looking absoutely 'right'.

There is also that same, unmistakable Caroline Charles 'look' about her evening clothes. Again, it is the choice of fabric that sets her ball gowns apart. There are the stripes and the bright patterns; the taffetas and the velvets for winter, the silks, the silk taffetas, the lace and the satins for the summer. Her style is classic, particularly designed to show off the figure – typical is the velvet and taffeta ball gown with the princess line that flatters the waist and hips. She will mix her fabrics too, as with her chiffon and velvet dress for the 'black tie' dinner. The evening jackets again will 'go' with everything, but then that is to be expected. After all, that is the success of Caroline Charles.

OPEN   Monday to Saturday 9.30 am to 5.30 pm (Wednesday until 6.30 pm)

# Cartier

■ 175 NEW BOND STREET                                493 6962
  W1Y 0QA
  (*Jewelry, including watches*)

Cartier's is a blissful shop. It is filled with sublime delights. The shop itself is as grand as can be, and is staffed by those who really do know what they are talking about. It has always been so, and thus always peopled by the discerning.

Cartier design and make beautiful jewelry, as they have done since the Second Empire in France – since 1847 to be precise. They have kept meticulous records of every piece they have ever made. Today, when working on a new jewelry collection, as they do every two years, Cartier look to their archives for themes – at the time of writing, these are animals, pearl, gold, and gold and diamond. Take the animal theme which is represented by the panther, 'the queen of all animals, a symbol of triumphant, sensual femininity'. It appeared first in 1919, then again in 1935. A panther bracelet was made for the Duchess of Windsor in 1952, a necklace in 1979. In the present theme, the panther is

28

stalking everywhere, from the most realistic form to the abstract. The panther graces their necklaces, in gold, on a five-link chain, in the clasp; it is there on a bracelet in diamonds and sapphires with emerald eyes, even lurking over a watch. There are brooches and rings where *pantheras pardus* hold a sapphire in their paws or mouth. The panther becomes a leopard in the abstract jewelry with gold or platinum pieces set with white or yellow sculptured pavé diamonds, cabochon sapphires and onyx spots. Then there is the whole range of panther watches with their distinctive gold-link bracelets, sometimes flecked with stainless steel, that has the sensual movement of its namesake.

The same, retrospective view is taken by Cartier for their exceptional watches. There is the fine, limited edition of the Pasha's Watch, modelled on the original made for the Pasha of Marrakesh in 1933. His requirements were diverse, something special for the evening, but waterproof. Today's equivalent, fashioned out of a single gold ingot, shows the date, month, moon phase, and leap years, even a second time zone. Then there are the Santos watches with their distinctive screw-heads based on the first ever wristwatch which was made for the famous Brazilian balloonist and aviator, Alberto Santos Dumont, in 1904. Another is the tank watch, whose bracelet resembles the impression of a tank-track in the ground. There can be few more beautiful possessions than a Cartier jewelry watch in gold, with a hexagonal or rectangular face, with either a jeweled or pearl bracelet.

Everything made at Cartier is instantly recognizable. Their work is particularly fine and delicate, especially the joints in all their pieces, whether the links of a bracelet or a high jewelry necklace. The high jewelry also comes in collections and, as its name implies, is even more especial than that of the theme collections. There is also a selection of antique and old jewelry, but all from Cartier. A special service that they offer is to redesign and make up any piece of jewelry to a customer's taste. With their meticulous records, they can also remake any of their original pieces to order.

Le Must de Cartier collections are beautiful adjuncts to the Cartier jewelry. They have continued as they began in the Twenties with creations in enamel, gold, silver and leather goods. Here are the lighters and pens, the leather wallets and luggage, even silk scarves. Often a lighter or a pen will reflect a Cartier theme; the screw heads on a silver lighter like the Santos watch, the three gold rings crossed on the tops of the pens (fountain, ballpoint and felt tip) and propelling pencils. The Cartier deep burgundy house colour is much evident in their leather handbags, wallets and luggage and the like, although there is a new range of fawn and blue to make a change, while the silk scarves are polychrome and correspondingly bright.

There is also a scent, predictably called Le Must de Cartier.

Another distinguishing feature of Cartier is their display. Here, within the carved, panelled rooms, there are cabinets, each of which contains items with a single theme. The high jewelry has a room of its own, where the pieces are shown on a Louis XIV ormolu table by any of the staff, all of whom are qualified jewelers in their own right. There are flowers everywhere and that, quite simply, reflects the pure quality of the place.

OPEN    Monday to Friday 9.30 am to 5.30 pm, Saturday 10.00 am to 4.00 pm

# Chanel Boutique

■ 31 SLOANE STREET                               235 6631
  SW1
  (*Scent and boutique*)

■ 26 OLD BOND STREET                    493 5040/5171/5270
  W1

Coco Chanel loved camellias. She also loved gold and pearls and the natural colours of beige and black, with a touch of white. She decorated her apartment in the rue Cambon (above the Paris shop) in her favourite colours, and mirrored the walls. Today, each Chanel shop (like the two in London) is decorated in those same colours: a sand-coloured carpet, black fittings and mirrored walls. Where there is a basement, there is a replica of her iron staircase. There is always a bowl of white lilies in the foreground of her shops. The staff are all dressed in black (dark blue for the summer) with a touch of white. They all wear a camellia.

Coco Chanel was an innovator. It was she who put women into trousers and comfortable jersey, and 'liberated them from the corset'. She created that indispensable 'little black number' and the neat, close-fitting hat. It was her scent, Chanel No. 5 (her lucky number) in its clean-cut bottle, that set the fashion for all fragrances to come. The look she created in the Twenties has lasted, amazingly little altered, to the present day, even after her death in 1971.

Today, Karl Lagerfeld (see page 106) is designing for Chanel in very much the same genre as the founder. He has taken that 'spirit' of the House which made Chanel famous in the past, and reinterpreted it for the present (some even say that this is his best work). The formula worked in the past, and it appears to work now. His collections of coats, suits, day and evening dresses, shown twice a year, are still very classical, invariably with some particular Chanel feature: the gilt buttons with the logo (the buttons with the Coco profile are new), a length of chain sewn into the lining of a coat so that it hangs better (and for show), a 'little black number', plain or trimmed with white or adorned with a black camellia, often a bow. He uses the Chanel favourite fabrics, wools and jerseys, cashmeres and silks, with velvet and organza for the evening. The blouses of silk, crêpe de Chine or satin generally have something of Chanel woven into the cloth. Lagerfeld also designs new collections of costume jewelry for Chanel, again with a predominance of pearls and 'gold'.

It was a particular trait of Madame Chanel to dress up everything with her jewelry. Typical were her leather belts, often adorned with chains; even more typical are the quilted, evening hand-bags in silk with their gold chains and Chanel adornment. Madame Chanel was also the first designer to develop the toe-cap of women's shoes. Although the heels change with fashion, it is a measure of Chanel's success that the beige and black (what else?) shoes look as smart today as they did 50 years ago. They have, of course, many other styles of shoes, particularly evening shoes.

Chanel fragrances, for both women and men, are legion and are led, as they always have been, by Chanel No. 5 (the original bottle is in the Museum of Modern Art, New York). There are the odd items for men too, like their silk ties and the fine, 5-ply cashmere sweaters. The cashmere scarves are unisex.

A special feature of Chanel is that everything is beautifully wrapped in black-and-white boxes adorned with their logo. The

31

*vendeuse* (and the doorman) all complement the rather sophisticated air of the place. Chanel is a smart boutique whose strength
lies, as it has done for over fifty years, in its understated elegance.

OPEN    Sloane Street – Monday to Friday 10.00 am to 6.00 pm,
        Saturday 10.00 am to 5.00 pm; Bond Street – Monday to
        Friday 9.30 am to 5.30 pm, Saturday 10.00 am to 4.00
        pm

# Charbonnel et Walker

■ ONE THE ROYAL ARCADE                              629 4396
  28 OLD BOND STREET
  W1X 4BT
  (*Chocolates*)

■ 2 KNIGHTS ARCADE                                  581 3117
  SW1X 7QP

Chocoholics have the Prince of Wales (later Edward VII) to thank
for Charbonnel et Walker, for it was he who persuaded Madame
Charbonnel to leave the Chocolate House, Maison Boissier in
Paris, with her considerable knowledge and expertise to set up (at
his expense) with a Mrs Walker the Chocolate House de
Charbonnel et Walker de Paris, Londres. The Prince of Wales, it
is said, had another reason to bring her to London that was not
entirely to do with chocolate.

Today, the main shop is at the mouth of Royal Arcade near the
bottom end of Bond Street and set behind an enticing bow
window, where there are more calories to the square inch than
anywhere else in London. All of their chocolates are hand-made
in Charbonnel et Walker's own factory, made in the traditional,
Victorian moulds (you can even have your own moulds made
up, at a price). Most of the chocolates are made from the original
recipes of the founders, so what started out as 'French taste',
dark, bitter chocolate, is now considered typically English.

What distinguishes Charbonnel from other chocolate houses is
not just the variety and quality of their chocolate, but the
packaging and service as well. They prepare boxes for all
occasions. There is the 'Drawing Room' selection of bittermints in
metre-long boxes of red and white, or an assortment of chocolates in their typical, white boxes, *boîtes blanches* (these make
excellent trout or salmon fly boxes when lined with green baize).
The 'After Dinner' selection are Charbonnel's Edwardian mints
(discontinued during the First World War owing to the shortage
of tin foil), their new Mocha Batons and chocolate orange and

chocolate ginger sticks. The 'Boxes at the Theatre' are either in floral paper or the silk covered 'hatboxes', and Charles Heidsieck champagne-flavoured truffles even come in an edible chocolate champagne bottle. It is a vain hope that the paper cups do not rustle, so keep them for the interval. Chocolate cartouches and croquettes flavoured with lemon or mint are for the 'Shooting Party' while the 'House Party' selection consists of peppermint creams, nut fondants, maple brazils and the like. To start children off young, there is the 'Nursery' selection with delights like *langues de chat*, dairy fudges, Parisian creams and a Duck Box.

Where Charbonnel go to town is with their 'Anniversary Boxes' in a round *boîte blanche*. These are filled with the usual assortment of chocolates but with a message spelled out in lettered chocolates, foiled in gold, ruby or silver. These can be of any size although there is a limit of 10lb (in a 3-foot-diameter box) for the verbose. There are ten ribbon colours to choose from, or a combination of colours for the regiment or the successful horse owner. They pride themselves that they can make up any kind of box to order.

Another service of Charbonnel et Walker is to keep a record of each client's preferences, 'Your delights are others' dislikes.' So, if you have a new love or are staying for a weekend at Chatsworth or with the Hardly-Humans, it is best to check if they are 'registered' first. Alternatively, it is worth buying a sample 1½lb box to mark your own card in the hope that this will work in reverse.

Charbonnel et Walker have a good standing-order service and send, first class (what else?), their client's chocolates all over the world. Gift wrapping is free except at Christmas but, as their chocolates keep well, you can forward plan.

OPEN   Monday to Friday 9.00 am to 5.30 pm, Saturday 10.00 am to 4.00 pm

# Charles Jourdan

■ 39–43 BROMPTON ROAD                                      581 3333
   SW3
   (*Shoes and boutique*)

There was a time when Charles Jourdan were known solely for their beautifully made, high-heel shoes and straight boots for the older woman. While all those safe, dependable styles are still there, they have now branched out into younger, more exciting and fashionable shoes.

At Charles Jourdan, there are two collections a year that more or less reflect the current fashion. There is always something new. Where the styles and heel-heights remain basically the same ('flatties' to high stiletto), it is the leathers and fabrics that make the changes. Apart from the finest leathers and suedes in every colour, Charles Jourdan use other exciting materials such as metallic-stamped leather in cubist designs, velour, crêpe-de Chine, even denim, plain or decorated with rhinestones. Evening shoes are still very much their speciality, including those more traditional, high-heeled shoes that are so exclusive that they are even numbered. The complete range of men's shoes is the same meld of the traditional and the exotic; from what every trendy young Frenchman is wearing to the straight chukka boot or tasselled shoes in crocodile or ostrich.

Complementing these shoes is a whole range of women's and men's clothes, predictably with a strong French influence. Charles Jourdan also have their own fragrances: for women, *L'Insolent*, and for men, *Un Homme*. It is no surprise to find the widest possible selection of luggage, in every size and variation – from a wallet and key-holder to a suit-holder and a golf-bag. It is attractive with its leather trim and tough, in a grey PVC.

Charles Jourdan has recently been completely reorganized and redecorated with elegant pale greens and greys. They also offer a special service for the woman executive who is too high-powered or busy to shop. She can either make an appointment and visit outside shop hours for the complete, personal service, or alternatively, she can send in her size and an idea of what she is looking for and they will take the appropriate shoes and clothes to her office. Charles Jourdan has certainly come a long way since those court shoes.

OPEN    Monday to Saturday 10.00 am to 6.30 pm, (Wednesday until 7.00 pm)

# The Chelsea Design Company

■ 65 SYDNEY STREET                                                   352 4626
SW3 6PX
(*Women's designer fashions*)

The Chelsea Design Company is Catherine Walker, just as Catherine Walker is The Chelsea Design Company, the founder, owner and above all, designer. Hers is a new-found reputation,

and talent, for creating distinctive day and evening dresses, but a reputation that is no less deserved for its comparative newness.

At the Chelsea Design Company, there is an especial, almost indefinable, elegance about Catherine Walker's clothes. But it is not just the clean, uninterrupted full-length line that comes with perfect cutting that sets her apart. Nor is it that precise shape that slims and stretches the body around the waist (what the better fashion photographers show in silhouette), anymore than it is her refined choice of colour, or structured use of fabric that make her clothes so individual. It is *all* that together, *and* the designer too.

Catherine Walker is French. The French instinctively have a feel for clothes, and know how to wear them. It is something they are born with, just like Brazilians and the samba, or the West Indian ability to play cricket. Catherine Walker has a doctorate in philosophy (aesthetics, what else?), and the advantage of no formal fashion training. Thus, it is her very Frenchness that is translated to her clothes, whose design appears as if created totally in the mind, rather than developed on paper.

There are two complementary sides to the Chelsea Design Company, couture and ready-to-wear. Catherine Walker has a large following for both. She enjoys that special relationship with her clientele, specially for the couture, who partially provide the 'sounding board' for new and exciting ideas, which in turn translate to the ready-to-wear. As there are only comparatively few examples of any one design, and they can be fitted, they too can virtually be considered as bespoke. Thus, she has no need to, nor does she, follow fashion, but merely interprets what she feels is right for the season, tempered by the choice of fabric and colour. Predictably her colours are mainly matt, dark and sophisticated; blacks and navies, dull pinks and the like, with brighter colours for the evening. Her fabrics are generally matt too, like the baratheas and tweeds, the woollen *crêpes* or the sericeous materials of taffeta, chiffon, duchesse satin, *crêpe romain* and Jacquard silks. A new departure is suede and the softest of leathers.

Catherine Walker has exactly the same approach to all her clothes, whether it is a savagely tailored, tweed riding coat with a velvet collar or a suit, a cocktail dress or an evening dress (there are no separates, for the mere fact that they are two pieces means that the full-length line is broken). As most of her clothes are limited editions, there is plenty of scope for flamboyance, even eccentricity. She will let herself go for Ascot; for the evening there are often sequins, ostrich-feather sleeves or the like, even a bustle, or maybe a peplum waist on a coat-dress.

This is a wonderful shop; honest too, for it is the clothes that flatter, not the assistants. Like Catherine Walker's clothes, there are no frills in the shop, just plain bleached wood as a neutral foil. With anything from the Chelsea Design Company, the wearer is sure to walk tall.

OPEN   Monday to Saturday 10.00 am to 6.00 pm

Under the same name and banner of (and a short step from) the Chelsea Design Company, is their children's shop at 46 Fulham Road (you cannot miss it as it is in a former greenhouse). Unlike its parent, the style here is totally quantifiable being very English (Kate Greenaway and sailor suits to the fore). Here, too, are the smocked dresses and Liberty prints that have been worn, and handed down, for generations, as have the Fair Isle sweaters and the long shorts that never date. There are also dresses for girls who have outgrown the children's department – for those around 14 or 15 depending on maturity, but have not quite reached the next stage.

# Cordings

■ 19 PICCADILLY                    734 0830/0868
   W1
   (*All foul-weather kit and all men's clothes*)

Cordings have been selling waterproof clothing from their shop in Piccadilly for as long as anyone can remember, in fact much, much longer for they were established in 1839. There have been many generations who have been thankful for Cordings and their invention of rubberizing cotton and canvas. Their weatherproof coats were, and are, legion; while their Newmarket boots (also their invention) were found to be pretty useful. No doubt Stanley found his inflatable raft from Cordings pretty useful too in his search for Livingstone.

Cordings has always been like a breath of country air in the heart of London's West End. In the basement, are the ready-to-wear tweed jackets and suits that all have that 'look' that comes with quality and the cut that makes them equally smart in town, or at home in the country. There, are corduroy trousers, nicely tailored despite being 'off the peg'. The brogues and other country shoes are made exclusively for Cordings by Edward Green.

There are sweaters and shirts on the ground floor, while the Cordings 'speciality', coats of every description, are on the first floor. They still manufacture their rubberized cotton rain coats in various colours and in two weights, the lighter single-ply and the heavier double-ply. They have their own style of the traditional mackintoshes and trench coat, the style of which never changes whatever the current fashion. Then there are the other more unusual coats like the Inverness Capes (favourite wear of Edward VII) and Raglan coats in loden cloth (perish the thought of a loden mantle here in this most English of places). What is equally special to Cordings are their covert coats, with or without the brown velvet collars.

There is a preservation order on the whole shop interior, not that the owners would dream of changing fine Scotia-baronial-hall-oak-panelling or the old fittings, for they do go rather well with the tradition of Cordings.

OPEN   Monday to Saturday 9.00 am to 5.30 pm (Thursday until 7.00 pm)

# Cosmetics à la Carte

■ 16 MOTCOMB STREET                                        253 0596
   SW1X 8LB
   (*Bespoke make-up*)

When Christina Stewart and Linda Saunders first opened their shop in Motcomb Street, they prepared all their cosmetics themselves in the basement. One night, a policeman spying them carefully weighing out the different powders on scales and balances, ordered a raid on the premises, suspecting a bomb-making factory. It did not, however, take long to convince the 50 officers of their mistake. Today, their life is more gentle with a factory over the river in Battersea.

This is a veritable cosmetic workshop, where both sides of their business complement each other. On the one hand, they provide a comprehensive make-up service (lessons, re-style, wedding, photographic and the like), and special skin-care for the face, eyes, hands and feet. On the other, they manufacture and sell a complete range of their own skin-care products and make-up.

As proprietary cosmetics become increasingly expensive, it is important to find exactly the right tones and colours first off. Cosmetics à la Carte do just that – after all, if you try on clothes before you buy, why not cosmetics? Here, they are totally flexible with all their products. As no two clients' needs are ever the same, each is given individual service. They will tone their foundation creams and face powders to suit, and when totally satisfied, they can repeat the order exactly. The quantities are kept small for all their products which makes them flexible and also reduces the need for excessive preservatives. There are some 150 different shades of eye-shadow and the same number of lipstick colours. They keep meticulous records of all their customers' colour formulas, so once agreed, it is simple to re-order by post.

The skin-care product list is equally comprehensive with cleansing and toning creams, nourishing and moisturizing creams, body care and sun care. There is also a range of aromatherapy treatment products based on natural extracts from flowers and herbs. The oils come from a special supplier in Grasse, the centre of the French cosmetic industry.

The shop itself is bright and feminine, if not a little sugary, with pink walls and turquoise chairs. At least the constabulary will not make the same mistake twice.

OPEN    Monday to Friday 10.00 am to 5.30 pm (Wednesday until 7.00 pm)

# Courtenay House

■ 22–24 BROOK STREET                                629 0542
W1
(*Country clothes and lingerie*)

■ 188 SLOANE STREET                                 235 5601
SW1

If *Burkes Peerage* is to be believed, 'the Courtenays are one of the illustrious races among the English nobility.' Although unconnected with the Courtenay family (or indeed Devon, their seat and earldom), the founder of this House of Courtenay, Peter Collins, took their name for his shops in 1972 as he believed that it gave exactly the right impression for what he wanted to achieve. To him, and possibly his clientele as well, the name conjures up a sense of solid Englishness (despite the Courtenays' tenth-century aristocratic French origins), of the tradition of the country, and of quality. Within these high ideals, Courtenay House has two sides to its business, country clothes and lingerie.

Courtenay House is especially proud of its country clothes, although for country perhaps you should read 'county'. They are invariably smart. Where the fabrics, all wools, cottons, linens, silks and leather are entirely natural, the colours are neutral. Their style is as ageless as they are traditional. Nostalgia, not fashion, dominates the design which is generally taken from Twenties and Thirties (even Edwardian) fashion books, never a jot later. So traditional are these designs that some of their clothes, like their Fair Isle sweaters, appear to have been abandoned by the last Prince of Wales after playing golf at St Andrews or, in the case of their stylized Norfolk jackets, to have come straight from a *grande battue* at Sandringham.

These country clothes are all manufactured in Courtenay House's own factories which, without the middleman, means that the clothes are good value for money and that quality is guaranteed. Tweeds are woven to their patterns – one clever design factor is to make up sweaters in exactly the same wools as those used in their tweeds. Hand-in-hand with this old-fashioned image is traditional workmanship. The sweaters are hand-knitted, blouses have pearl buttons, and everything is hand-finished.

The same refined Courtenay taste is applied to their lingerie, that is, as they claim, 'not remotely overtly sexual'. It is carefully selected from the top European manufacturers or made up to their own exclusive designs. Again, there is the attention to detail, like the range from Florence where they do the best embroidery. A measure of how discreet and sophisticated their lingerie is can be gauged by the fact that even the shyest of men can shop for their womenfolk without a hint of embarrassment. Courtenay's also carry ranges of colour coordinated beach wear.

The two shops are well set out, decorated in soft, restful colours with interesting window displays. The changing rooms are spacious (most London shops require you to possess the skill of Houdini to change your clothes) and the staff are predictable, being a mixture of Euro-chic and dependable English. Everything can be gift wrapped (at no extra charge) or is parcelled up in stiff carrier bags bearing their logo – Courtenay in gold on a deep red background.

OPEN    Monday to Saturday 10.00 am to 6.00 pm

# Crolla

■ 35 DOVER STREET                                                    629 5931
  W1
  (Avant-garde *men's fashions*)

When opening a new shop, it is a somewhat novel (and brave) approach to decide that your future clients will want something new and somewhat controversial long before those clients know it themselves. Crolla, or to give him his full name, Scott Crolla, did just that when he founded his shop in 1981. He decided to cater for the young, stylish and leisured man who needed a conventional suit for his conservative job. For him, Crolla took the 'uniform', the pin-striped or grey worsted suit, and re-tailored it to give a sharper look. He then applied the same technique to the rest of the man's wardrobe, shirts, ties, even socks — flamboyance that was only just acceptable to the establishment. As Crolla describes it, his 'is an arrogant disregard for good taste.'

While he still sells those suits, he has now branched out into more unconventional clothes. An innovator, Crolla was the first to make up garments in furnishing or unusual fabrics. Suits, jackets and trousers now come in an amazing range of colours and textures — from a comparatively sober tartan to high-camp gold *lamé*. Now he will design a fabric and then design the garment to fit that fabric rather than the other way around. His shirts are unusual; ties are interesting without being too loud. Boxer shorts, pyjamas and dressing gowns come in a variety of fabrics, socks can be monogrammed to order. There is even a line in alpaca coats which, surprisingly, sell throughout the year, regardless of the weather.

Crolla also make and sell women's clothes in much the same vein as the men's — cosmopolitan in unusual fabrics.

The shop itself is ramshackle, thrown together with a mixture of styles and tastes. One of the changing rooms is like a gigantic, wooden pepper-grinder (the type that Italian waiters use in restaurants to grind pepper into your wine!)

Crolla is certainly not for everyone, but then not everyone is young, stylish and adventurous.

OPEN   Monday to Saturday 10.00 am to 6.00 pm


# Cutler and Gross

■  16 KNIGHTSBRIDGE GREEN                           581 2250
   SW1X 7QL
   (*Ophthalmic opticians, and sunglasses*)

Cutler and Gross, or, as their friends call them, Graham and Tony, are opticians. They are also designers. They happen to be very good at both. Thus, their clients tend to be those who are fashion conscious (many are also fashionable in their own right as well).

Here, there are between 20 and 30 basic shapes of frames, so with the variations of thickness and colour, the combinations are limitless. To them, a frame is a speciality in itself. It has to be comfortable, to suit and fit the client, hold the lenses and to look good as well. Most of their frames are straightforward, but they all have that little 'extra' something that makes them absolutely right. Cutler and Gross offer a good service too. As all their frames are made in their own workshops by their own staff, from the eye-test to the finished, bespoke pair of glasses takes only one week. Also, they will design and make anything on request, given enough warning.

They have a big line in sunglasses, again in high fashion with that same Cutler and Gross distinctive look and quality (the frames are light and comfortable and fitted with safety plastic lenses). They also stock the famous Italian Persol sunglasses.

The shop itself is elegant, bright and cheerful, decorated in grey with partial 'looking-glass' walls. For an appointment, it is best to telephone first. If you are still not convinced about their spectacle prowess, just watch the better television, go to the cinema or the theatre, or attend a fashion show. The best spectacles are bound to be theirs.

OPEN    Monday to Saturday 9.00 am to 6.00 pm

# James Drew

■  3 BURLINGTON ARCADE                          493 0714/9194
    W1
    (*Women's shirts, skirts, coats and dresses*)

As you walk down Burlington Arcade, you can tell at a glance from the façade of their shop exactly the type of clothes that James Drew sell: it is a pretty shop selling pretty clothes. James Drew was originally a man's shop, and, although their clothes are fiercely feminine, there is still something of the man's tailored look about the whole collection. Here you will find the pure English classic look, but with a style of its own: the silk shirts for day and evening, the cotton shirts with their pie-crust collars, the ruffled blouses, and every other variation of shirt and blouse. There is a timeless quality about their clothes. Where the styles remain fairly constant, the changes are rung with new and exciting fabrics. They also sell the accessories: safe, sensible hats, cashmere sweaters, belts and gloves, especially those with suede palms and knitted backs. The jar of polychrome balls on the table is not full of sweeties, but of elasticated cuff-links.

James Drew also have exotic night wear – remember Lauren Bacall in *Sweet Bird of Youth*? She was wearing James Drew silk pyjamas. There are men's style silk dressing gowns in fine, Paisley silk.

Up the narrow, spiral stairs are jackets and skirts. Their men's tailored appearance is further compounded in the choice of fabric. There are mannish tweeds and velvets. Many of the skirts are made from men's tie material. But then that is hardly surprising, James Drew is now owned by Turnbull and Asser (*see* page 153).

OPEN   Monday to Friday 9.00 am to 5.30 pm, Saturday 9.00 am to 1.00 pm

# Alfred Dunhill

■  30 DUKE STREET                            499 9566
    ST JAMES'S
    SW1Y 6DL
    (*Pipes, tobacco, men's fashions, watches, luggage*)

At the turn of the century, it was shrewd of Alfred Dunhill, a harness-maker's son, to site his small tobacconist shop in Duke Street, off St James's, for there in the heartland of the better London clubs he picked up all the passing trade as members walked between their clubs. Later he acquired a pipe workshop in the adjacent Masons Yard. He also had a business selling motoring accessories, both clothes and leatherwork. A philanthropist innovator/inventor, he introduced for the one-armed ex-servicemen after the First World War, the Unique lighter, the first rollerlighter with a horizontal flint wheel. His maxim throughout was that everything in the shop 'must be useful. It must work dependably. It must be beautiful. It must last. It must be the best of its kind.' Today, Alfred Dunhill Ltd is still in the same shop, selling the same kind of products – tobacco, pipes, leather, clothes and gadgets, and its founder's maxim still holds good.

Dunhill still has a fine reputation for pipe tobacco and cigars. They have their own tobacco mixes, including a 'mixture of the month'. They can make up a mix from any number of tobaccos specially for a customer. Once the customer is satisfied, the selection is then entered into 'My Mixture Book' and the customer is given a reference number for re-ordering. Every Dunhill pipe is hand-made in their own factory from the best briars and, apart from the quality of workmanship and its 'feel', it is instantly recognizable by the white spot at the top of the mouthpiece. If a customer cannot find a suitable pipe among the hundreds of styles in stock, then one can be made specially to order in their factory. Upstairs in the humidor room (past an interesting collection of pipes), are the cigars. The room, with its vaulted ceiling, sandalwood cupboards and heavy iron and brass gates to the store-room, is somewhat reminiscent of a Cuban cigar-dealer's shop. They stock the leading eight brands of Cuban cigars and one of their own. All cigars are kept at a constant 65°F and 75% humidity, including those bought forward by their customers.

Those gadgets (defined in the dictionary as 'small mechanical appliances or accessories') certainly live up to the Dunhill maxim. Their Millennium (dictionary definition: a thousand years, future age of peace and prosperity) watch is a fine combination of British design and Swiss craftsmanship. The range, which spans 70 variations of strap, face and shape, is led by the Elite and crafted in solid gold, or a combination of gold and steel with an open-link bracelet. The range of pen sets (fountain and ballpoint pens and propelling pencil) is equal to the watches in beauty and design. At the top end of the range are the Dress sets, either gold or silver plated, 'lined' or 'barley' finished. The lighters have come a long way since the Unique model, although Dunhill has re-introduced a modern version as a celebration of the original. There are many features that make their Rollagas, Dress and Gemline lighters special. All three come in many different styles and finishes, in gold plate, silver plate, steel and lacquer, or in combinations of them all. The same almost engineering approach has gone into their jewelry, most of it in gold or silver.

It is not a misnomer to describe the Dunhill handcrafted luggage as endearing (enduring too). There are four comprehensive, matching collections of leatherwork: the Oxford, the black Cambridge with its contrast stitching in brown, the super-soft lambskin and Warwick, each differing only slightly in style or in leather. There is everything from a key-holder to a large suitcase, from a briefcase or attaché-case to a wallet. Each item is carefully thought out; for instance, the wallets are designed in several sizes to take pounds, dollars, francs or yen.

Dunhill guards its name fiercely and no less so than with its full range of men's clothes. These are classic clothes, designed of the country and for the country. The basic tailored styles vary little, but only use luxury fabrics such as cashmere, wool, silk and linen. The Dunhill blazer in finely woven wool is timeless, and is especially good for travelling as it refuses to crease. The discreet Dunhill logo can be detected in surprising places – on the bottom of their silk ties, on belt buckles, sunglasses and spectacle frames, scarves, cuff-links, polo shirts and the like.

The shop is open and inviting and has recently undergone what a former U.S. Ambassador termed 'an element of refurbishment'. Each area has its own distinct smell, be it rich tobacco, fresh leather or Edition, the latest of Dunhill's own toiletries for men. The staff are knowledgeable and enthusiastic about what they sell. It is still a family firm; the founder's daughter, Mary Dunhill, is the President, and his grandson, Richard Dunhill, is the chairman.

OPEN    Monday to Friday 9.30 am to 5.30 pm, Saturday 9.30 am to 4.30 pm

# Victor Edelstein

■ 3–4 STANHOPE MEWS WEST                              244 7481/2
SW7
(*Women's designer clothes*)

If you were to attend the most elegant, international dance of the season, the chances are that the evening dress, or indeed dresses, that would stand out, would be those designed by Victor Edelstein. However, those initial, arresting qualities of an Edelstein dress are not superficial (there are never any unnecessary frills or adornments about them), merely a beautiful line, where the 'material is cut around the body', with a perfect fit. Nor does he mix his fabrics. The choice of fabric, however, goes through phases, changing with the season and the collection; maybe a floppy silk or a duchess satin, or a velvet for the winter. Although usually plain, the textures often vary, sometimes even pleated. His colours are generally strong, vivid and punchy, although there is usually a black number in the collection.

Victor Edelstein has two collections a year consisting of day and evening dresses, coats and suits, from which his clients can choose. Being couture only, anything can, of course, be made up in a choice of fabric. Edelstein also enjoys doing 'one-offs', especially wedding dresses. Belts and hats are within his field too. Ideally, he likes to have at least three fittings for each garment; it can be done in less, but then he is a perfectionist who guards his reputation for a good fit. Although he does not like doing it, overseas clients can get away with just one fitting and the dress is then sent on by air freight. Either way, depending on the season, it takes about three weeks to complete an order.

With such flair as a designer, care for detail and a workroom to match, it is no wonder that Victor Edelstein's dresses and coats have such arresting qualitites.

OPEN    Monday to Friday 9.30 am to 5.30 pm or thereabouts
Appointments only

# Edina Ronay

■ 141 KING'S ROAD                                    352 1085
SW3
(*Designer hand-knit sweaters*)

There are 2,000 outworkers knitting for Edina Ronay, that is
4,000 needles clicking away every day of the week and probably
the weekend as well. This little army producing her range of fine,
hand-knitted sweaters make her the largest, and not to say the
most exclusive, designer in Britain today. The quality and
workmanship are matched by the use of the very best yarns —
cashmere, silk, silk and wool, angora for evening wear, sometimes fine cotton.

Edina Ronay (the daughter of the restaurant critic, Egon
Ronay) has developed her distinctive style slowly. She began
selling antique clothes (by way of St Martin's School of Art, the
stage and fashion modelling); then, inspired no doubt by the
Thirties and Forties sweaters on her stall, she went into producing
her own hand-knits. She still produces those classic sweaters,
like her range of Fair Isles and cables, but her new collections are
now bolder in design and use of colour.

Edina Ronay has recently gone into designing co-ordinated
clothes with the same verve as shown in her sweaters, with that
touch of sophistication, style and femininity combined with the
best use of materials and colours. These are complemented by a
range of leather belts and bags by Il Bizonte, shoes by Patrick
Cox and a few hats from Viv Knowland.

There is a nice, cosy atmosphere about the shop, with bright
sweaters arranged on stripped pine shelves and Welsh dressers,
a positive oasis in what is now a rather seedy King's Road. Edina
Ronay can also be found in Harvey Nichols and Liberty's.

OPEN   Monday to Friday 10.00 am to 6.00 pm (Wednesday
until 7.00 pm), Saturday 11.00 am to 6.00 pm

# Etienne Aigner

■ 6 NEW BOND STREET                                  491 7764
W1 0AR
(*Leather accessories, luggage and classic clothes*)

At Etienne Aigner you can find everything that can conceivably
be covered in leather, from the smallest tooth-pick to the largest

46

cabin trunk. Also everything, but everything bears the Etienne Aigner logo, a stylized horseshoe in the shape of an A. Nothing is spared – neither the watch, the propelling pencil, nor even the tools in a leather case for the up-market artisan. However, they are as proud of their logo as they are of their workmanship, especially in their fullest range of luggage.

German in origin, Etienne Aigner have applied their country's precision and practicality to the design of their luggage. The range is comprehensive, smart, durable and functional. They specialize in smaller luggage, with cases the maximum size for aircraft hand luggage, such as a neat 'management case' which is a pair of 'saddle-bags' that slip over a briefcase, just right for a short business trip. They also do a leather Gladstone bag that would delight a Prime Minister of any party. Then, there are larger suitcases, again in leather sold singly or in a complete set. The ultimate, however, made only to order (allow six months for delivery), is a three-piece set of traditional pig-skin luggage with brass trim and wooden struts. For the really serious traveller, there are three sizes of hanging trunks. Not quite in the same league as the pure leather cases, but none the less smart, is their luggage range of placticized linen with leather trim.

Aigner have their own leather spray polish to keep all the leather luggage in good condition. They also have a luggage repair service, but only for their own cases.

Besides this luggage and logoed leatherwork is the Etienne Aigner range of clothes, for both men and women. These clothes take on a rather classic, European look in tweeds and flannels, silks and wools. Also, there are the leather logoed accessories with a fine range of belts, shoes and handbags.

The shop is predictably smart with the logo woven into the carpet and stamped on the leather furniture.

OPEN   Monday to Friday 9.30 am to 5.30 pm, Saturday 9.30 am to 5.00 pm

# William Evans

■ 67a ST JAMES'S STREET                         493 0415
SW1A 1PH
(*Gunmaker, shooting accessories*)

Unlike most specialist manufacturers and shops, gunmakers are all equally polite about their competitors (and that is not only because most of them carry each others' used guns). Instead, they just maintain, in the politest terms, that the choice of gunmaker is a matter of preference which is solely up to the customer. However, there are many who swear that William Evans is the best.

William Evans think so too, for why else would they have always called their two guns *Best* – the 'Best' Sidelock and the 'Best' Boxlock. For these, there is a two-year waiting list, as indeed there is for the William Evans rifle. This rifle is built on the original Mauser action, in every calibre, and with the special features of a low-mounted scope sight and an adjustable drop trigger. All guns and rifles can be engraved with anything the customer wants or with William Evans' own pattern.

Alongside their guns and rifles, William Evans has a wide range of shooting accessories. Their own cartridges come in three types, *St James's HV* for those high birds, *Pall Mall* for maximum penetration and minimum recoil, cased in paper or plastic, and for those prone to headaches, the *Marlboro*, also cased in paper and plastic. There are cartridge belts and four types of cartridge bags (canvas, pigskin, hide lined and unlined). This is the place to find cartridge-bag slings in regimental colours (allow two weeks delivery). Everything for the gun is there too: cases, gun covers and slips, also cleaning kits.

Knick-knacks and clothes form an increasingly larger part of the gunmaker's business, and William Evans is no exception. Best among a wide selection of flasks and whistles, hats and scarves, shooting-sticks and spotted handkerchiefs are their shooting socks with splendid ribbed tops.

This is a shop of fine, old-fashioned service. Small repairs during the season are done on the spot, literally, and as quickly as possible. Full servicing takes longer. Guns and rifles can be stored for a nominal charge. The staff, led by one of the directors, Mr Bodger, all give the impression of knowing all there is to know about guns: what is more, they probably do.

OPEN    Monday to Friday 9.00 am to 5.00 pm
        No credit cards

# Eximious

■ 10 WEST HALKIN STREET                                    627 2888
  SW1
  (*Monogrammed items and presents*)

This shop is a prime example of little acorns growing into big trees. However, this little acorn did have all the advantages of being the right acorn to start with, planted at the right time, and deluged with the right fertilizer in the form of the flair of the founder, Mrs Val Cridland, the marketing expertise of her husband and later, a timely injection of dollars from the retiring United States Ambassador and his wife, Mr and Mrs John Louis.

Eximious sprouted quite by chance when Mrs Cridland found a firm to embroider a monogram on a suit-bag she had had made for her husband. From there, she began supplying her friends with other monogrammed bags, then their friends, and then the friends of those friends, and so the business grew. That same, hugely expanded friendly network of customers still exists, and to an extent is the strength of the shop today. For the first five years, Eximious existed solely through their mail-order catalogue, somewhat truncated by comparison with the present one.

Since the majority of the items for sale in the shop can be monogrammed or (perish the word) personalized, at first sight it appears to be largely a 'present shop'. Although everything here would make a handsome present, the idea is more to sell attractive items that will enhance a pretty room. Furthermore, the majority of items are not just decorative but practical as well. Items in the house and garden range are just that little bit more special than their competitors': the moiré silk photograph frames have little bows on the top, the candle carriers and shades are either printed or have a cut-out pattern. Customers' photographs of their choice can be made up into a tray or a set of place mats. They even have such indispensable items as a table planner for working out the placement at dinner and special tongs for opening bottles of champagne. Sewing and embroidery are well represented with tapestry bags, their own design of cushion canvases, and bobbin stands. The range of china and glass is special with such delights as ceramic flower bricks, loving cups and white bone-china toothmugs. Monograms, names, messages, even houses, can be engraved on their glass. The choice of glassware, though small, is adequate where the best are the carafe and glass, various decanters and tankards, tumblers, goblets and champagne glasses. There is a mass of leather desk accessories – look out for the heavy sellotape dispenser that stays put on the desk-top when pulled.

Although more and more items are added to their list annually, Eximious still stock all the original lines. Nothing, they believe, is more boring than to find something is discontinued when it needs to be replaced or added to. Eximious matching luggage is available in green and red, blue and red or black and camel. There are suitcases of every size, in light, heavy-duty waterproof nylon with zips. There are also bags of every size, shape and description, from the original suit-bags to sponge bags, plus bags for everything that could conceivably (or not) need a bag – tennis-racket bags, golf-shoe bags, shirt bags, even a bag to hold cassette tapes.

Men are well catered for here with such essentials as brushes, flasks and cigar cutters – Eximious also deal in nostalgia by marketing the old Royal Yacht range of men's after shave and hair lotions. Monogrammed socks and towelling bath robes (indeed, the towels themselves), for both men and women, are another Eximious speciality. There are also a few items and clothes for children too.

Apart from a few things, like the luggage and glassware, everything is made by outworkers – small specialist suppliers making to a high standard, always ready to take on a new idea or copy some antique. Monogramming and engraving generally takes around two weeks depending on the time of year (see the catalogue for times of other items).

The shop itself is like an overcrowded, decorative drawing room – the staff are also decorative, young, and efficient. They are generally friends of the family and all work as a family of friends which makes for an undeniably genial atmosphere. Their long-standing customers would doubtless endorse the English translation of their Latin name: 'excellent, distinguished, eminent'.

Their catalogue comes out twice a year.

OPEN    Monday to Friday 9.30 am to 5.30 pm, Saturday 9.30 am to 2.00 pm

# C. Farlow and Company

■  5 PALL MALL                                           839 2423
   SW1Y 5NP
   (*Fishing tackle and country clothes*)

There was a time when the game fishermen stocked up on their kit at the fishing-tackle shop nearest to where they were fishing. Today, fishing is so expensive that they cannot afford the time or risk not finding the right equipment so they now arrive fully prepared – hence the increasing popularity (and necessity) of shops like C. Farlow and Company, Pall Mall.

Farlows has a worldwide reputation of only selling the best (for many, their shop is the first call after arriving at Heathrow Airport). Although they do have everything for sea and coarse fishing, they specialize in game fishing. Selling the best equipment they naturally stock Hardy rods (*see page* 79). Apart from Hardy, they also sell Bruce and Walker rods and make their own split-cane rods. At any one time, there are over 100 different reels to choose from. Again, Hardy reels are the best, but they also stock the well-known Shakespeare reels, and for big-game fishing they have the full range of Penn reels from America. Also from the U.S. is the tackle from Orvis.

50

Everything, but everything, is here for the fisherman (and woman). There are over half a million salmon and trout flies for sale at any one time. They have every alluring trout fly (tied mostly in Africa) for every occasion, while their salmon flies are tied to their own specification by a small army of outworkers. If you fancy tying your own flies, then there is everything here for that too, from a moleskin to a peacock feather. They consider that the hand-made canvas and leather Brady fishing bags are the best, as are the Wheatley fly-boxes. Everything, including clothing, can be repaired here. If there is anything in the way of fishing tackle that Farlows do not have in stock, which is unlikely, then they will always find it. Farlows have bought the famous gunmaker Cogswell and Harrison, and, though they do not sell guns (except for air-rifles), they do have the whole range of shooting accessories, from cartridges to cartridge belts, from dog-training kits to decoys.

Further up in Royal Opera Arcade is Farlow's clothing shop. Here there is every conceivable form of clothing to keep out the cold, the water, the weather (rain and sun), the midges and anything else that might spoil a life out of doors. Apart from their practicality, many of their clothes have a certain chic about them too, especially for those women who like to dress up for shooting. For them, there is a whole range of Loden coats, capes and skirts from Austria, or the practical British Loofy range of waxed coats and overskirts with tartan linings.

Farlows have the largest selection of Barbour (fashionable for some, practical to them) and also Puffa quilted jackets and flotation waistcoats. Although comparatively expensive, there is also the Gore-tex clothing which, despite being synthetic, still 'breathes' (put less delicately, it allows the wearer to sweat).

There is rack upon rack of tweed, corduroy, moleskin and cavalry twill in every style of jacket, plus-fours, plus-twos, breeches, skirts and trousers. There are socks for shooting, gloves for shooting and mittens for shooting, in fact everything for the shooting man and woman.

Here is the ultimate selection of boots and what nanny termed 'sensible' shoes. The prize for the last word in wellingtons must go to the French, leather-lined *Bottes Le Chameau*. Also from France are the Aigle boots generally considered superior to the British boot in design. The ubiquitous Hunter green wellies are here in force, including the Royal and the Crown (some even claim a self-cleaning sole); also a good supply of waders by Ocean. Nothing by way of country footwear is forgotten. There are Derriboots and fur-lined Arctic boots, stalking boots and shooting shoes.

Both the fishing tackle shop and the clothing shop are purely practical (Farlows' only concession to decor is to have their name woven into the carpet). The staff are all qualified to advise on everything but will do so only if invited. Those who fish are by nature gentle souls (when fishing or thinking about fishing) and this is equally true of Farlows. For nearly 150 years, customers have been saying 'I'm sure Farlows will have it.' They have made absolutely sure that they do.

OPEN Monday to Friday 9.00 am to 5.00 pm (Thursday until 6.00 pm)

# S. Fisher

■ 22–23 and 32–33 BURLINGTON ARCADE       493 4180/6221
W1
(*Cashmere sweaters, waistcoats*)

S. Fisher, named after Sam Fisher the octogenarian founder, has the benefit of two shops in Burlington Arcade, the men drawing the low numbers at 22–23, the women the high at 32–33. Despite their numerical difference and gender, they still have the same, high-quality knitwear in both shops.

At the men's shop, they are the specialists for lightweight sweaters. For these plain or designer sweaters, they use such exotic or unusual yarns as single-ply cashmere, silk and cashmere mix, alpaca, even sea-island cotton. Besides these, Fisher's, of course, have every other weight and design of sweater like the Shetland and the lambswool. Alongside this miscellany of sweaters are other miscellanies; fine cashmere scarves, wool socks, including, they claim, 'the finest sock in the world' by Pantherella, and underwear from John Smedley. Fancy silk and wool waistcoats are another Fisher speciality (still cut by the octogenarian Sam), that would delight any member of Pop (the Eton Society) or lesser mortal.

Besides the regular sweaters in every weight and yarn, the women's shop stocks high-fashion designer knitwear. Again, they specialize in cashmere. They have cashmere capes and jackets and their sweaters run the whole gamut of weights: single-ply, 2-, 3-, and 4-ply, then the thicker 6-ply, going up to the fabulous 10-ply.

This is very much a family shop with three generations still working there. Despite its tiny size, it does not appear cramped; perhaps it is that that gives both shops their easy atmosphere.

OPEN Monday to Friday 9.00 am to 5.30 pm, Saturday 9.00 am to 4.30 pm

# J. Floris

■ 89 JERMYN STREET  930 2885
SW1Y 6JH
(*Fragrances and soap*)

'He who frequents the perfumer's shop and lingers even for a short time,' wrote the philosopher Seneca, 'will carry with him the scent of the place.' Just so today when you visit the House of Floris, for there you will find just as exotic a blend of scents as Seneca ever experienced in Rome in the first century AD.

Through seven generations and over 250 years, Floris has enjoyed a considerable reputation as 'purveyors of the finest English flower perfumes and toiletries', from the same address in Jermyn Street. Here, they sell their own products exclusively, made in their own factory to their own unique formulas. There are soaps of every size (including one in the giant Floris bowl that floats), perfumes and toilet waters, everything to scent the bath, essence, salts and gels, talcum powders and dusting powders, even scented drawer liners. These are available in straight flower fragrances, such as Voilet, Jasmine, Lavender, Lily of the Valley,

53

Lime, Rose, Sandalwood, Stephanotis or Wild Hyacinth or a blend of two or more of these fragrances, like the latest Edwardian Bouquet, based on Sandalwood with Hyacinth and Jasmine or Florissa, a veritable summer garden of 'Rose, Lily of the Valley, Syringa, Jasmine and Iris with the oil of Madagascar and woody amber notes'. However, not every item is available in every fragrance. Useful, are the room sprays and perfume vaporizers (essence that evaporates from cardboard rings on a light bulb) and the drawer sachets, also their special pot-pourris.

The men's fragrances are masculine: No. 89 for Men (named after their original address) and Elite. These come in a combination of most of the usual toiletries like shaving soap, aftershave, hair lotions and colognes.

There is everything to go with these fragrances and toiletries, both in the bathroom and the bedroom. For the perfumes and toilet waters, Floris have a lovely selection of atomizers and bottles which they will fill for their customers. Some are antique, some modern like those in Lalique crystal. There are also Chinese cloisonné enamel boxes filled with solid perfume. Brush sets and combs, for both men and women, come in every material: real ivory (when available) and simulated ivory, even shagreen inlaid ivory, real and simulated tortoiseshell, also silver. Brushes, whatever their provenance, can be rebristled here. The shaving brushes made exclusively for Floris, in ivory, or simulated ivory, with the finest badger hair come in five sizes. Some, like their razors, have exotic handles like horn or lapis lazuli. Toothbrushes, with the finest bristles, are similarly mounted with bone, ivory or cloisonné for something special. To complete the Floris bathroom is a range of Floris towels and bath robes, either in blue or pink.

This is a nice shop, and efficient too. They keep records of all their customers' particular likes so they can repeat an order. Any of their ranges can be altered to suit; for instance, a toilet water or fragrance can be made stronger or weaker. Everything can be gift wrapped, free of charge, in their distinctive blue and gold colours, all gold for Christmas. All items can be sent through the post, with a sliding scale of postal charges (free over £50).

This is an undeniably grand shop. The Spanish mahogany fittings were made for the Great Exhibition in 1851. There are always fresh flowers around. Everything looks grand too. The staff are courteous: not for them a 'Hello' or a grunt that serves in most shops as a greeting, but a crisp 'Good Morning, Sir' or a 'Good Afternoon, Madam'. There is a memorable touch of nostalgia in the custom of laying your change on a velvet covered plate, placed on the counter.

OPEN    Monday to Friday 9.30 am to 5.30 pm, Saturday 9.30 am to 4.00 pm

NOTE Next door is James Bodenham and Co which is owned by Floris, but run as a separate entity. Here are the products outside the Floris range, like their complete range of natural cosmetics, loose pot-pourris, preserves and vinegars. There are also essential and massage oils and natural Apple and Vitamin E soap, so natural that it is even wrapped in brown paper.

# Fogal

■ 36 NEW BOND STREET          493 0900
  W1

■ 51 BROMPTON ROAD          225 0472
  SW3
  (*Stockings*)

The idea of having bespoke stockings is somewhat ridiculous, particularly as there is nothing, but nothing, in the way of stockings that cannot be found at Fogal, in either of their shops in New Bond Street or Knightsbridge.

Here, Fogal sell everything, but everything that covers a woman's nether-regions (in some cases above as well), from simple knee-high socks to those sophisticated stockings in the sheerest silk or cashmere. Arranged around the spokes of a Catherine wheel to the front of the shop, is a good representation of what is on offer. In ascending denier-order, from 11 (the sheerest), through to an opaque 40, and rising to 60, the tights are knotted like so many hanks of wool, the colours of each particular style to be seen at a glance. In all, there are well over 100 fashion colours, although not every stocking is available in every colour; like the sizes, most go from extra small to extra-extra large, some even with custom fits for long legs or wider hips.

There is seemingly no end to the variations of pantihose and stockings. They are plain or ribbed, matt or 'sheer and shimmering with satin sheen'; they are decorated, studded with rhinestones or painted with silver or gold. They come with patterns incorporating bows, birds, polka-dots, and stripes, and fishnet, many with fantasy finishes or lace: they come with seams – seams down the front or seams in rhinestones. Some are made for warmth, like their winter pantihose (smooth, ribbed or braided) in natural fibres such as silky cashmere or pure merino wool. Then there are the exclusive, self-supporting, garter-top stockings, in the same exciting range of patterns and colours, or alternatively, the same in a pantihose, with cut-outs for the

55

garter-belt effect. There are bodystockings of every description, from opaque to fine (one so transparent that it is called nude).

Fit is as important as design. To be technical, many of their stockings have a percentage of spantex or elastine for the perfect fit with no wrinkles. All stockings can be tried on in a large changing room. Fogal stockings are always changing with fashion, but old favourites can be reordered in three to four weeks.

Socks are another Fogal speciality. Again, here is everything for both women and men, plain or patterned, in every fabric from nylon to a silk-cashmere mix with over 80 colours to choose from. They are all cleverly displayed in a book on the counter, showing each sock and the spectrum of its colours.

The Fogal shops are identical. The design is purely functional rather than aesthetic. However, the brightness of the poly-chrome stockings matches that of the staff, all of whom take a great deal of trouble with their customers. Here, shopping for a pair of stockings takes on a whole, new meaning.

OPEN    Monday to Saturday 9.30 am to 6.00 pm (New Bond Street until 7.00 pm on Thursday; Brompton Road until 7.00 pm on Wednesday)

# Fortnum and Mason

■ 181 PICCADILLY                                                734 8040
W1A 1ER
(*Department store, provisions, wine*)

'There was never such a Derby Day as this present Derby Day!', wrote Charles Dickens, a regular Fortnum and Mason customer. 'Never, to be sure, were there so many carriages, so many fours, so many horsemen . . . so many fine ladies in so many broughams, so many Fortnum and Mason hampers, so much ice and champagne . . . Look where I will, I see Fortnum and Mason [hampers]. And now, Heavens! All the hampers fly wide open and the green Downs burst into a blossom of lobster-salad!' But then those Fortum and Mason hampers were nothing new. Cases of their preserved food had been sent to Wellington's officers in the Peninsular War; later, lucky officers in the Crimean War received their marvellous fare, often with a request that the F&M be left off the cases to stem the 'undue leakage of luxuries during the voyage.' Fortnums hampers became an indispensable part of every war, including the First World War; they even returned the compliment of Mrs Pankhurst's brick being hurled through their

window by sending her a hamper to Holloway jail. Such courtesies were nothing new either, for Fortnums had been supplying fine food to valued clients since Mr Fortnum teamed up with Mr Mason in 1707, and from that same address in Piccadilly.

Although designed today to be eaten in less bellicose circumstances, Fortnums picnic hampers and boxes are no less welcome. There is a choice of five different menus, four of them in boxes, which come with disposable plates, knives and forks, and one in a hamper, the exotic Midsummer's Day Picnic Hamper for two, in a proper wicker basket (returnable against a deposit). Picnic boxes and the hamper should be ordered at least 24 hours in advance from the provisions department. There are also four different fitted picnic baskets (*sans* food and wine), hand-made of the famous Somerset willow with its golden 'glow', for two, four or six people, fully kitted out with everything, including a woollen rug and the essential corkscrew.

But those hampers are just a small part of the Fortnum and Mason food hall that covers the whole of their ground floor. The provisions department is an Epicurean dream, with such delights as sides (and packets) of wild, Scottish, oak-smoked salmon, various hams, Stiltons and a special truckle Cheddar (besides dozens of other English and Continental cheeses). Here, too, are the pâtés and terrines, and general charcuterie. A great feature of Fortnums food is their attractive packaging, especially their ceramic pots, which are filled with such delicacies as caviar (Beluga and Sevruga) or goose liver terrine with truffles (*foie gras*). Also in these ceramic pots, that really can be put undecanted on the table, are the house specialities, like gentlemen's relish, English and French mustard, jams and marmalades. In keeping with their tradition of fine, preserved foods in tins, Fortnums have such exotica as quail in jelly, goose quenelles and duck à *l'orange*, while their tinned soups, like spiced turtle or lobster bisque, are famous. Fortnums have their own bakery on the premises for bread and cakes (they can make, and specially decorate, any cake to order). There is a wondrous selection of hand-made chocolates, truffles and crystallized fruits; also fresh flowers, rare (and ordinary) fruit and vegetables. With twenty-seven different teas, including one blended specially for New York tap water, and six coffees (fresh ground or beans), and all those special sauces, bottled fruits and the dozens of different biscuits, there is not much (if anything) in luxury food that is not here. Fortnums wine list is comprehensive and chosen for everyday drinking rather than for laying down. However, they can store wine for their customers. They are particularly strong on champagne, with their own house champagnes, which include a rosé.

The basement is given over to china, glass and silverware. Here there are all the top china manufacturers, with the likes of Herend, Minton, Dresden, Royal Crown Derby. These makes, as with their glass suppliers, like Waterford Crystal and Baccarat, are, of course, available elsewhere, but many of the patterns and styles are exclusive to Fortnum and Mason, such as the hand-painted Satsuma porcelain from Japan. Most of the china and glassware is sold at the recommended retail price and so no more expensive than anywhere else.

Although Fortnum and Mason are best known for their luxury foods, there is a complete women's fashion department on the first and second floors. The styles are classic, elegant and traditionally English, with stockists like Jaeger but enlivened with a dash of Jasper Conran (*see page* 104), Alistair Blair and Paul Golding. Beside the fashion are some of the leading perfumers, also the lingerie and millinery departments, including Frederick Fox (*see opposite*) and Viv Knowland, and Christian Dior sunglasses. On the second floor is the Schumi hairdressing salon and women's accessories (handbags and shoes), and their own range of tapestry luggage, with other makes. Upstairs on the third floor is the menswear department. This is largely dominated by the Italian, Ermenegildo Zegna, with some English suits from Chester Barrie and Tommy Nutter (*see page* 123), who also has a selection of smoking jackets. Particularly stylish is their exclusive cashmere dressing gown lined with madder silk, and the loden blouson from the Italian Sicons. Beside the menswear is the stationery, toys, and children's wear.

The fourth floor is divided between the antique furniture department with its predominance of mainly eighteenth-century mahogany and walnut, and the St James' Restaurant. The restaurant serves morning coffee, lunch (a set menu and à la carte), and Afternoon Tea, when there is usually a pianist. The Patio Restaurant on the mezzanine above the ground floor, does a light lunch, and of course coffee and tea. Below, on the Jermyn Street level, is the Fountain Restaurant with its Soda Bar for cream teas and, every schoolchild's delight, those marvellous sundaes, piled into deep glasses, with such evocative names as maple dipper, banana boat and Jamaican sun. This restaurant is open until 11.30 pm.

There is a dependable feel about Fortnum and Mason: the plush, red carpets, crystal chandeliers, and wooden statuettes of Mr Fortnum and Mr Mason. The senior sales staff all wear black morning coats (red for Christmas). Outside, the clock strikes on the hour, the two founders bowing to each other before returning to their alcoves to an eighteenth-century air. Their horse-drawn van will deliver special purchases, free of charge, within central London, but generally deliveries are made by a motorized van, whose range covers all London postal districts.

How lucky it was that Mr Fortnum teamed up with Mr Mason.

OPEN    Monday to Saturday 9.00 am to 5.30 pm

# Frederick Fox

■ 87–91 NEW BOND STREET                                    629 5706
W1Y 9LA
(*Women's hats*)

Frederick Fox can make a woman's hat better, and quicker, than anybody in his employ. This is not entirely surprising since he has reached the pinnacle of his trade as a designer through the milliners' workrooms in Sydney and London, and later, through the salon of Langée. Nor is it at all surprising that Mr Fox is the Milliner Royal, creating hats for seven members of the Royal Family (including the Queen, Queen Elizabeth the Queen Mother, the Princess of Wales and her new sister-in-law, the Duchess of York). As with his Royal clients, Frederick Fox spans the generations, making hats that suit all ages, all faces, all over the world.

Although Frederick Fox does have a shop with his own ready-to-wear collection of hats which he shares with the designer, Murray Arbeid (169 Sloane Street, London SW1, telephone 235 5618), and his hats are found in most of the major stores, his extra special couture hats are created in his third-floor salon in Bond Street. Here in an elegant, panelled room, often among a muddle of hats on trees, Frederick Fox receives his couture clients. Their hats are all strictly 'one-offs', designed and made usually with a particular outfit in mind or more often several outfits (it is as well to bring the outfit, or at least a swatch and a sketch of the design).

There is an unmistakable Frederick Fox hand-writing about all his hats. Seemingly a frustrated sculptor, he creates that clean line and often novel shape that so distinguishes his hats, be it a wide-brimmed straw hat, an amusing platter or the flimsiest cocktail number. He is strong on veils and the more sophisticated trimming, like ostrich feather. However, he does go overboard for Ascot, which he terms 'nervous breakdown time'. As he keeps in close contact with all the leading fashion designers, both in London and abroad, Frederick Fox makes sure his hats are compatible with the current trends.

His customers are naturally all very special to him. Such is his relationship with many of them, that they will just telephone him and ask for someting for a specific occasion. As he knows their taste and preference, he produces something suitable, sight unseen. Frederick Fox enjoys designing hats for weddings, particularly the hat for the bride's mother. Although what he creates for her will not outdo the bride, it will, like all his hats, most certainly be noticed.

Appointments essential

# Garrard

■ 112 REGENT STREET
W1A 2JJ
(*Jewelers*)

734 7020

Those who saw the BBC television series 'Royal Heritage' may recall that splendid scene of the Crown Jewels being cleaned by a bevy of old women in the Tower of London: the Imperial State Crown polished on the lap of one, the Sceptre scrubbed by another. It was just another day in the life of (and one of the many services rendered by) Garrard, The Crown Jewelers. Garrard claim that they are family jewelers, but jewelers with a difference (besides being the Crown Jewelers, they look after most members of the Royal Family as well).

This long-standing connection with the Royal Family began in the mid-eighteenth century with Frederick Louis, Prince of Wales of 'Poor Fred, he's dead and there's no more to be said' fame. Fortunately for Garrard's founder, George Wickes, Frederick Louis patronized him (before his untimely death) by ordering vast, silver centre-pieces, candelabra, and the like. This tradition for fine, even exotic, silverwork is as strong today as then. To the back of the shop is the silver room, where there is a fine display (possibly the finest in London), of antique silver. Where all the great silversmiths are usually represented, Garrard makes a point of keeping many of their own pieces. The same goes for silver-gilt. They also sell second-hand silver, like Thirties tea services, which cannot be classed as antique.

Garrard's modern silverwork is complete. For example, there is a sample of every single pattern of tablewear, kept in drawers reminiscent of an old-fashioned, egg-collector's cabinet. Here too are the sconces and candelabra, punch bowls and, the ultimate in TV dining, a silver Lazy Susan, and of course much, much more. In their special commissions department, Garrard can make up anything in any material. They are equally famous for their trophies (the America's Cup and the Santori Golf Trophy to name but two), as they are for their sculptures (mostly horses) and their models of ships, planes and other military hardware. Of course, there is nothing (save price), to stop anything being made up in gold. Every conceivable type of jewelry can also be made by the special commissions department: regimental brooches and the redesigning of old-fashioned pieces being a speciality.

Alongside this splendid silverwork is the collection of Garrard's jewelry, both modern and antique. The modern jewelry is consistent with its traditional design and both old and modern settings. Here are the diamond and pearl necklaces, the rubies and the sapphires, also some more contemporary pieces like animal brooches or gold, snake-like necklaces. The antique collection is always changing, but often incudes such exquisite pieces as a tiara or strings of pearls.

Like most things at Garrard, their watches are of the finest brands, and represented by 15 Swiss manufacturers like Patek Phillipe, Vacheron Constantin and Blancpain. They also have something that is just that little bit different such as their own watches, some with reversible faces, others with a moving face. (They also repair all makes of watch.) Besides these modern watches, Garrard has a fine selection of antique pocket watches, also clocks, both modern and antique, including carriage clocks.

A new venture (at the time of writing) is the gift department: here, for example, are rather imaginative presents that are definitely in the luxury bracket: amazing boxes, photograph frames and the like made from lapis lazuli, malachite or the intriguing and unusual wood stone from California (what can hardly be classed as gifts, but are none the less pretty), and practical items like a full porcelain dinner service (Garrard will monogram or 'crest' anything), or fine porcelain pieces from the better factories like Herend, Flora Danica or from Dresden. Here too is the crystal with the well-known names of Lalique, Edinburgh and St Louis.

The staff, all of whom have been trained in every department but specialize in one, fit neatly into the somewhat decorous surroundings. Poor Fred would still be at home here, buying his trophies and centre-pieces. No doubt he would have recognized the eagle console table in silver in the style of William Kent on the stairs, doubtless he would have admired the amazing, fantasy castles, in 18-carat gold and set with diamonds by William Tolliday.

OPEN    Monday to Friday 9.00 am to 5.30 pm, Saturday 9.30 am to 5.00 pm

# The General Trading Company

■ 144 SLOANE STREET                                      730 0411
   SLOANE SQUARE
   SW1X 9BL
   (*China, glass, leather, toys, furnishings, presents*)

The General Trading Company looks very grand from the outside. The white, wrought-iron balcony that supports all four Royal Warrants spans the front of the four, tall Victorian buildings which make up the shop. It is pretty grand inside too; the well-proportioned rooms, the wide staircase, and the grey of the walls as soft as the carpet. Then there is the staff, all of whom patently appear to enjoy working there among friends. Against this superior foil is all that they sell, well set out in twelve separate departments. However diverse these departments may appear in their goods (it is, after all The *General* Trading Company), they are united in the fact that everything throughout the shop is chosen for its aesthetic quality, workmanship, practicality, or because it is just plain fun (very often it is a combination of all four).

Since its founding in 1920, the GTC, as it is affectionately known, has become an institution with its many customers. Over the years, the affianced have set up their new homes through wedding lists there, just as generations have shopped there in the knowledge that they will find exactly the right present, or an indulgence, even a necessity, for themselves.

On the first floor is the eighteenth- and nineteenth-century furniture, pewter-ware and framed prints. Here the stock is obviously transitory. Less transitory, in that it can be re-ordered, is their reproduction furniture – dining tables and chairs, chests of drawers, revolving Georgian bookcases, and the like. In what they aptly term 'Modern Living', is the contemporary designer furniture, although the sofa, called the Burnham (reasonably priced), is redolent of a more comfortable age. Here, almost more than anywhere else in the shop, GTC has the chance to demonstrate its true aestheticism, *vide* the ceramics by John Hinchcliffe and Wendy Barber. Here too is the linen department, complete with painted beds and a very fine line in silk bedspreads.

There is a strong Oriental flavour to much of the shop; the Indian dhurries and fabrics in cotton, wool or silk by Shyam Ahuja are a prime example. Downstairs are the products of the better shopping in Eastern bazaars, with Indian brasswork,

Turkish kelim cushions, papier mâché objects and coral from the Philippines, plus whatever else their buyers' wanderings bring in. Next is 'Modern Gifts' which is self-explanatory in that it sells all those presents and things that one would really use rather than store up for the daily's next Christmas box. Typical are the Perspex ice-buckets, bottle-coolers, jugs and glasses, even a plastic shooting stick and picnic rug. Woven into these fairly standard items are those frivolous knick-knacks, just right for that little extra, fun present. Typical is the sweatshirt which has printed frog's eyes that light up and blink, and which croaks when its tummy is pressed.

With a limited space on the ground floor, the stationery section is somewhat cramped, but that means their stock, like the cards and wrapping papers, the marbled photograph albums and Billingham Filofax in canvas and leather, is all carefully chosen. The same is true of the toys (their suppliers are all members of the Toy Makers Guild). Here are such excitements as a wooden Noah's Ark, complete with animals but no *homo sapiens*, proper rocking-horses and rocking woolly sheep (most decorative).

The garden department is seasonal, in that it has the fullest selection of dried flowers in winter, and a fine selection of garden furniture (note the Lutyens' bench), terracotta pots and tools in summer.

'Traditional Gifts' is a serious department with everything that complements a smart London life and the house in the country. Here is the leather (the photograph albums and visitors' book, the waste-paper baskets and umbrella-stand), and the ceramics (the Limoges toothmugs, initialled, of course, and the Herend ducks). Here too is what is on every wedding-list by the dozen, place-mats and trays, *cache-pots* and *jardiniéres*.

To the rear of the shop is a large, well-lit space for everything connected with 'elegant eating'. Here is the glass and china, the cutlery and the table linen. Fine dinner services of all the leading makes, including Spode, Royal Worcester, French and Italian porcelain, also Herend, are laid out around the walls. There are also drawers full of dozens of samples of services for which they can take orders. The same applies to the glass and crystal. Samples are set out on shelves, like the complete sets of Baccarat and Waterford, crystal from Austria, and their own special Royal Brierley. Crystal bowls, another wedding-list essential, are there in profusion.

In the basement is the kitchen department where there is everything for the 'well-bread' kitchen. Here necessities like saucepans and dishes and aprons and the like all have a dual role: not only are they the best, they look attractive too. Justin de Blank has the concession for the restaurant which opens, with the shop, for breakfast at 9.00 am and serves tea and coffee throughout the day until 5.15 pm (1.30 pm on Saturdays). His (J de B) is a predictably exotic lunch menu, that is eaten inside, or in the garden in summer.

Christmas is special at GTC. The staff in the shop doubles and it fills up with more Christmassy things, including Christmas decorations. There is a superb catalogue for mail order (the cost of which is deducted for orders over £10). Delivery, in their new bright yellow vans, is free within the London area for orders over £75, under is a nominal £2. Anything small can be sent by post.

The General Trading Company sells lovely things: it would have to be a very odd friend indeed (or relation) who could not be matched to a present from the GTC.

OPEN    Monday to Friday 9.00 am to 5.30pm, Saturday 9.00 am to 2.00pm
        *Christmas* 16 November to 24 December, Monday to Saturday 9.00 am to 6.00 pm (Wednesday until 7.00 pm)

# W. and H. Gidden

■ 15d CLIFFORD STREET                           734 2788
  W1X 1RF
  (*Saddlers, and all riding wear*)

Since 1806, six generations of experience and dedicated service of the Gidden family have earned them the reputation of one of the finest saddlers in the world today. They began as harness-makers, tanning and curing their own leather and making everything, except saddles, that could possibly be made of leather. Fifty years ago they began making saddles, so successfully that when the competition, like Champion and Wilton, and Whippy, went out of business they bought them out, but kept the name and the styles.

Today, a hand-made Gidden saddle is a unique possession. It will have been made from start to finish by just one man and it is a measure of their quality that any saddler who is Gidden trained has a passport to the job of his choice if he leaves. Bespoke saddles are made to fit the rider, often the horse as well, although the life of a Gidden saddle should be considerably longer than the riding life of a horse. Saddles 'off the rack' can be tried on a large wooden horse in the basement of their shop – they can also be tried on the horse if it is near one of the staff (Hertfordshire, Kent or Surrey). Saddles can also be part exchanged.

The range of Giddens' own saddles is complete, everything that horse or rider could possibly want. Here there is the Gidden

All Purpose saddle, various dressage saddles, eventing, military and polo saddles (they make the legendary Whippy Stegal Polo saddle). These are all crafted in top-quality hides, in three colours, on conventional spring trees and stuffed with new wool. Like the military saddles and harness, these can all be made to order in any combinations of leather. Beside the Gidden range, they also sell 'the best of the rest', like the full range of Stubben saddles, the Barnsby polo saddle and the Epic Endurance saddle for those demanding rides across open spaces. They also sell racing saddles (the best come from Australia, the lightest weighing a mere 8 oz).

No saddle or saddlery is too difficult for Giddens to make, in fact they welcome the challenge. They have made elaborate, presentation and ceremonial saddlery for Arab Emirates, even a complete set of harness for the Oman Mounted Camel Band, and a saddle made entirely in red leather for Zsa Zsa Gabor. The ITN crew who went to film behind the Russian lines in Afghanistan had a special donkey harness from Giddens to carry their heavy camera equipment. It is still in use there, doubtless for carrying ammunition boxes. They repair leatherwork too.

Giddens also stock every conceivable, and inconceivable, item that is remotely connected with the horse – they produce a useful and comprehensive catalogue (£2) for mail order. They also have the last word in 'hippo-chic' with matching rugs (initialled, coroneted or whatever), tail guards and leg bandages. Besides catering for the horse, the rider is well provided for too. Everything is there by way of clothes – hacking-jackets, breeches and boots (the complete range as per the Gidden Riding Boot Company), polo caps (helmets are old fashioned now) and hunting caps, crash-hats and racing silks. The 'County Uniform' is stocked – green wellies, thorn-proof jackets and padded waistcoats, not forgetting the leather-cornered hip-flask.

The shop is a veritable treasure-trove for anybody with horse-sense. That wonderful smell of new leather permeates from the woodwork like an old-fashioned tackroom. The staff are generally all horse-mad, the sort of girl that you have known since Pony Club camp.

There is something here for everybody: even the local antique dealers find their hippo-meters useful . . . for measuring statues.

OPEN   Monday to Friday 9.00 am to 5.15 pm, Saturday 10.00 am to 1.00 pm

# Giorgio Armani

■ 123 NEW BOND STREET                    499 7545
W1
(*Italian designer, women and men*)

There are no frills at Giorgio Armani, neither to his clothes nor to the shop. Everything is clean-cut and simple – even the two mannequins in the window have plain black balls for heads (often they are not even afforded the luxury of arms and legs) as it appears that nothing should distract from his clothes.

Giorgio Armani, as those interested in fashion know, is one of the most influential of today's designers. His is a special talent that, over the years, has produced a refined, elegant look that has almost become the symbol of the Eighties. His designs are for women who wear clothes as an adjunct to themselves, rather than clothes that take over the wearer. The fabrics he uses all 'work'. Not only do they complement the design but move gracefully with the wearer, while at the same time, flattering the figure. His clothes are narrow-cut, without a trace of unnecessary adornment (so much so that most of his suits are collarless). His colours are somewhat sombre, but that does not make them any the less exciting or fun to wear.

At Giorgio Armani, there are three distinct lines, lines delineated by price and age. At the top end is Armani, the couture collections that appear twice a year; then Mani, a distillation from the collections and less expensive, and the fun clothes of the Emporio Collection. Both the Armani and Mani collections have a definite continuity about their designs. As his clothes are so well cut, and the change in style and colour from collection to collection slight, everything co-ordinates especially well; even an Armani suit is a co-ordinating, rather than a matching, jacket and skirt.

The evening wear is exciting. Again he uses all the finest fabrics: the silks, the velvets and the chiffons. Here, there is often a throwback to the Twenties and Thirties with evening trousers and suits, and evening hats and berets to go with them. Some sparkle too, with rhinestones and/or sequins; typical is the simplest of blouses in grey, entirely covered with 'heat-sealed sequins'. The more expensive numbers are usually one- or two-offs. There is a range of jewelry too, predictably, in dead metal colours.

Downstairs is for men. Giorgio Armani in fact started designing men's clothes (hence the simplicity of his designs for women). Again, there are three distinct ranges of clothes: the couture, the G.F.T. (a distillation from the couture), and the Emporio. Exactly the same principle applies here with the whole range of suits and overcoats, jackets and sweaters, shirts and ties, even shoes, all tying in with each other to give one over-all appearance. For example, it is typical of Armani to put a sweater with a particular suit to dress down, or a shirt with the same suit to dress up. There is a bold use of fabrics, like the tweeds, camels and cashmeres. Trousers tend to be high waisted, pleated at the front, almost baggy, without a centre crease. There is also the full range of men's toiletries under the Giorgio Armani label. Men have Armani to thank for the blouson; his are either suede, leather or wool. The Emporio range is purely casual. Here are fun clothes, young and jolly. The range is mostly sportswear, track suits, jeans, polo shirts and the like, all with a strong Fifties overtone.

The shop is bright and as clinical as you can get with greys and blacks. There is a sparse feel about the place, clean-cut and direct. Unlike most shops, the clothes hang outwards (generally their entire stock) as opposed to sideways in rows. The staff are enthusiastic and patently proud of what they sell.

As Armani says himself, 'Dressing should be fun, a way of being more at ease and of feeling more attractive and confident.' His clothes do just that.

OPEN   Monday to Saturday 10.00 am to 6.00 pm (Thursday until 7.00 pm)

# Thomas Goode and Company

■ 19 SOUTH AUDLEY STREET    499 2823/4291
   W1Y 6BN
   (*China, glass and silver*)

It is almost a misnomer to call Goode's a shop, house would be far more appropriate (after all, did not Queen Victoria herself approve the plans when the founder's son, William Goode, added to the premises in 1876?). There is the same rich decor throughout all thirteen rooms, with fine embellishments of plasterwork and gold-leaf, painted ceilings and decorated Georgian friezes, vaulted rooms hung with chandeliers and tall arches, all perfectly preserved. So too is the pair of Minton elephants, seven feet high, with their gilded howdahs, standing on carved wooden plinths, beside the main entrance. Unique are the mechanical doors of the same era, that open when you stand on the mat which says 'Welcome'. And a welcome it is.

Goode's have a reputation of supplying only the best English and European china and porcelain. They also have a reputation for being very expensive, which is unfair, as, although they do sell some extremely expensive china and porcelain, they charge no more than the recommended retail price for anything. They give an unparalleled service that only comes with continuity; many of their suppliers have been with them for generations.

Each of those suppliers has a room, or a whole display area, devoted solely to its range of china. Some of the grander dinner services are displayed on Georgian dining tables for better effect; others are laid on hexagonal tables with mirror-divides that reflect each place setting. The choice appears limitless, with each supplier offering so many different services within a range, with wildly differing price tags. For example, side by side are two of the Minton collections, the Minton Gold and Haddon Hall. The former is encrusted in gold and is correspondingly expensive, the latter has a pretty, flower pattern and is comparatively inexpensive. The traditional patterns are always there, like Crown Derby's exotic Imari dinner service. As they will always keep stocks of everything they supply for the inevitable breakages, Goode's are loath to take on anything too *avant garde* or a new supplier that may be 'shaky'.

The Antique Room is undeniably special – ask to be let in as the iron gate is kept locked. Around the walls is an arched frieze, each arch with a different bird (from the exotic or mythical to an old owl or common magpie) on a gilded background. Like much of the china in the room, they were designed by William Goode, himself a fine ceramic artist. Here, they keep china and glass very much of that period, beautifully displayed on a dining table or in brake-front cases around the walls.

The rooms of English china match with each other, just as they do in their Staffordshire and Midland homes of manufacture, with famous names such as Wedgwood, Royal Doulton, Coalport and the aforementioned Minton and Crown Derby. Behind, are the Continental showrooms with such equally renowned names for their porcelain as Limoges, Bernardaud, Haveland and Gien from France, Villeroy and Bosch from Germany, and Royal Copenhagen from Denmark. So special is the Herend from Hungary that it takes prime position in the front of the shop. Goode's has the largest selection and stock of Herend in London, like the well-known 'Rothschild birds' dinner service.

Goode's are not just 'chinamen' of note, for they have an equally fine selection of glass and silver. Some of the chandeliers in the house are the original fixtures, the rest, both antique and modern, are for sale. However, Goode's can make up any chandelier, either copying an original or working from a photograph. There is shelf upon shelf of the finest crystal and glass. All the leading names are represented: the English Tudor and Royal Brierley, Irish Waterford Crystal, the Scottish Edinburgh and Stuart, alongside the famous French *verreries* of Baccarat, St Louis and St Lambert and, of course, Lalique. There is everything in glass that could possibly adorn a table, from a rose bowl to a salt cellar, a set of gilded glasses to a set of vodka glasses around a caviar bowl.

To complete the dining table, there is the complete set of silver cutlery and silverware. Goode's carry all the traditional English patterns, such as King's pattern and Queen's pattern, from a variety of the better manufacturers. Many of the silver, or silver gilt, canteens have been made specially for Goode's. Above the cases of silverware, the dishes and the candlesticks, the coasters and the pepper and salt grinders, is the finest collection in the world of *pâte sur pâte* vases.

Then, there are the rooms with lamp-bases (with shades made to order), designer rooms with looking-glasses and beautiful vases, rooms with clocks and rooms with presents, especially at Christmas. Where else could you find a porcelain owl with a four-foot wingspan?

The service at Goode's has always matched its refined, old-fashioned atmosphere. The staff are trained for six months in each department before they are allowed to serve a customer, and it shows (on Tuesdays, they open half an hour later to allow time for staff briefings on anything new in the house). Goode's will undertake special commissions, from engraving a salt cellar to decorating a vast dinner service with a monogram or armorial bearings. Their huge stock is stored in the cellars, where every piece sold is individually wrapped. They deliver free in the London area by their distinctive green antique van, or post smaller items (the larger packages go by surface carriers).

When it is time to leave the shop, those fascinating mechanical doors will open automatically and the elephants will still be there, as they have been for 100 years.

OPEN  Monday to Friday 9.00 am to 5.00 pm (Tuesday from 9.30 am), Saturday 9.30 am to 1.00 pm

# Green's

■ 34 ROYAL EXCHANGE                                    236 7077
EC3V 3LP
(*Seriously good wine merchant*)

This is a seriously good wine and cigar merchant with a seriously good wine list. But then they should be good; after all, Green's has been trading for 200 years within the City of London, mostly from the present address. The Edwardian, bottle-green façade of the shop, tucked into the the the northern end of the Royal Exchange (leave the statue of Baron Reuter to your back and advance), is indicative of who, and what, is on offer within.

At Green's, they love people. They love customers even more. Either way, they are only too happy to talk to anyone, whether they are after half a bottle of Gordon's gin or 20 cases of the best claret. They are led from the front by one of their directors, the ebullient Richard Parsons, though the rest of the troops are no less knowledgeable or helpful. The walls are lined with racks of their wine, exemplified in their catalogue (so good that it makes fine, vinous, bed-time reading).

Green's are especially good in the traditional areas of the wine trade: claret, burgundy, champagne and the fortified wines of France, Spain and Portugal, and less good on wine from other countries (although they do have more than a sample representation of all of the better wine-growers from California to Australia, the long way round). As with other merchants, they have also become shippers, which means that they buy (on the advice of a Lady Master of Wine and the choice of the directors) from the grower direct. The liaison between Green's and the grower is exemplified by the red and white burgundy from Maison Raoul Clerget, which, among many others, include the renowned (and reasonably priced) St Aubin, and the Chassagne Montrachet. With such a relationship between Green's and their growers, their wines become especially personal. They also have their own label, Floquet, of house champagne and cognac.

Very special on their list is the Bas Armagnac du Château de Lacaze, for which Green's are the sole U.K. importers. This armagnac, which comes in two versions, Armagnac de Lacaze and the superior Heritage Armagnac, is the only one available here that is produced from grapes grown in their own vineyards.

Although they would far rather sell wine for drinking, Green's also offer a complete wine and spirit investment service. They usually work an *en primeur* system, that is, buying claret while it is still maturing in the cask during the first two years of its life. When ready, the wine is then bottled and shipped (at the customer's expense) and, if required, stored at Green's own warehouse until ready to drink. There is, of course, no guarantee that the wine will continue to be a good investment, but there is always a good hedge for the private buyer: the wine can be drunk.

For a wine merchant, Green's has an exceptional selection of cigars. All the top Havanas are there, Bolivar, El Rey Del Mundo, Rafael, Punch, Partagas, Montecristo, Romeo y Julieta, H. Upmann, and the thin Ramon Allones. Add to that Green's special selections from Jamaica, Holland, Honduras and their own Swiss cheroots for probably the largest stock of cigars for a London wine merchant.

While it is best to come to the source, particularly with something as personal as wine, Green's wines, spirits and cigars can be ordered in their Champagne and Oyster Bar in the West End, also called Green's, at 36 Duke Street, St James's, London SW1 (930 4566).

Once you have been given a drink, the wine has been discussed and possibly bought, then there is always cricket to go on to. After all, that is just the kind of place Green's is.

OPEN    Monday to Friday 9.00 am to 5.30 pm, Saturday 10.00 am to 1.00 pm


# Gucci

■ 27 OLD BOND STREET                                              629 2716
W1X 3AA
(*Shoes and leather, presents*)

The green and red stripe in the Gucci colours is almost as well known as the green, red and white of the Italian flag. The stripe, in fact, represents a girth, a reference to Gucci's origins as saddlers from Florence. Florence is also the home of fine leather and leatherwork, so it was only a short progression for the founding Gucci to diversify from the tack-room to less equine products (although the horse still looms large in their designs).

Today, Gucci are still making fine leather goods, and much, much more besides, from the largest trunk to the smallest wallet, with plenty in between. Gucci luggage is a speciality. Cases, in pigskin or pressed leather with pigskin trim, come in all sizes with every kind of bag to match, particularly the suit bag – that better export from America. In an identical range are the leather and canvas cases and bags, called either GG Plus or Mignon, a specially treated canvas with the GG initials within a rhomboid design. Their selection of attaché-cases in such precious skins as crocodile, lizard, and other exotic leathers, must be one of the smartest out. But it is for their huge selection of handbags that Gucci is probably best known. Here are literally dozens of different styles, sizes and colours – navy, brown, black and Africa (beige). Again, these come in calf, crocodile, lizard or mignon (the treated canvas printed with their logo) with pigskin trim, often with a Gucci stripe emblazoned across it. Then there are the belts with the Gucci buckles, the wallets and note cases and, the last word in Yuppie chic, the Gucci Lefax binder.

Gucci are equally renowned for their enamel work, watches and jewelry. Here are the enamel, enamel and silver or gold pens, all with the Gucci stripe. The same goes for their collection of lighters; nor is there any mistaking where their gold-plated quartz watches come from with their famous Gucci stripe, their name or their logo across the face. Key-rings are another Gucci speciality with 'a cast of hundreds' to choose from, also money clips and cuff-links. Much of their jewelry goes in a theme. At the time of writing the theme is the crocodile, with its distinctive hide appearing in silver or gold on bracelets, necklaces, earrings and the like. Gucci also sell glass and ceramics.

There can be few shoes that are better known than the men's Gucci loafer, with its snaffle bit across the front. There are, of course, many other Gucci shoes (including a Gucci wellington boot, a Gucci tennis shoe, even espadrilles). Here too are Gucci clothes: the women's clothes, day and evening wear; men's, the usual range of cashmere jackets and flannel trousers (with, of course, much more in both ranges). What does stand out are the Gucci silk scarves, with dozens and dozens of patterns to choose from, and the widest selection of Gucci silk ties.

Although Gucci are now worldwide, not all their shops sell the same things. Buyers of each department are given a free hand, so the London buyers are catering solely for their own customers. The shop itself is predictably smart, with an international sales staff. They pride themselves on service and operate a customer-service department where anything bought at Gucci can be repaired. They have surely come a long way since those days of that founding Gucci in Florence.

OPEN    Monday to Friday 9.00 am to 5.30 pm, Saturday until 5.00 pm

# Hackett

- 65a, b and c NEW KING'S ROAD     731 2790
  SW6
  (*Complete gentleman's wardrobe*)

- 117 HARWOOD ROAD     731 7129
  SW6
  (*Formal wear*)

- 1 BOXHOLME HOUSE     736 0567
  NEW KING'S ROAD
  SW6
  (*Second Hand*)

These are the shops for those who really appreciate quality and recognize good value. Hackett's began by selling good, second-hand men's clothing – unlike women's clothes, bespoke suits that were built to last a lifetime (and beyond) do not date. When they (Jeremy Hackett and Ashley Lloyd-Jennings) found that they could not keep up with demand, they recognized a real market for new 'old' clothes and so began producing clothes based on the very best of the traditional styles. Within two years, they had established a clutch of shops around Eel Brook Common, one for new clothes, and two for second-hand men's clothes.

Here it is only tradition that counts. The cut of the suits and coats (perish the word 'sports-jacket'), is traditional – slim and stylish for the slim and stylish man. The tweeds are traditional, from a sensible green herringbone to screaming checks, all copied from old favourites and woven to their own designs. They have their own covert coats with velvet collars; even pure linen suits that would delight any pre-war colonial administrator or planter. There is also a good line in dinner jackets. Above all, the tailoring is traditional, carried out in their own factories. It is the attention to detail (traditional) that sets their clothes apart. The buttons are horn; the cuff-buttons open. The pockets are of strong cotton; there are buttons on the fly – not for them a new-fangled zip. On the whole, their traditionally minded clients are young, setting out in the City, the Army or the tweedy country. For them, Hackett fills the gap between the 'rack' and the bespoke tailor, with a price-tag to match. However, if your figure does not match that of a dashing rake out of a Disraeli novel, then Hackett will alter their patterns to fit at no extra charge.

To go with all these traditional suits and coats is a whole range of traditional shirts, sweaters, braces, ties, shoes and socks, even umbrellas. The sweaters, like the braces, come in various grand colours, Eton, MCC, Guards and the like, and also plain. The trousers, both corduroy and Cavalry twill, are cut narrow with a 'hunting-boot leg' in mind, although the flannel trousers are wider.

Tradition also prevails with the staff and their four shops. Each of the men's shops has the air of comfortable, rather sporty, Twenties Oxbridge undergraduate's rooms with blades, college shields and striped paper about the walls. The staff, despite their obviously slender years, all appear to be at home here and have the air of being the major products of minor public schools or the minor products of major ones. Each is courteous and efficient. At Christmas, like Fortnum and Mason, they don morning dress, but unlike F and M, they have proper stiff collars and their shoes are spit and polished.

The two second-hand shops still stock a rich variety of clothes. One has a selection of those well-built suits, plus-fours, boots, hunting breeches and coats, 'helmets – pith, one' and so on; the other specializes in morning dress and evening wear (if caught in London without a dinner jacket it may well be cheaper to buy an immaculate one second-hand than to hire an ill-fitting one for the night). Certainly both shops are worth a visit, if not to buy, certainly for interest. Besides a range of leather luggage, from a cabin trunk to a hair-brush case, there are such items as leg-of-mutton gun cases, old Hardy rods and reels, old gaffs and cartridge bags, even a partridge carrier and an immaculate pair of button spats.

If you are ever asked to stay in a very grand house in the country where your case is naturally unpacked for you, you can be sure that everything you bought from Hackett's will look entirely at home.

OPEN    Monday to Saturday 10.00 am to 7.00 pm


# Halcyon Days

■ 14 BROOK STREET                                           629 8811
   W1Y 1AA
   (*Enamel boxes, antiques and clocks*)

■ 4 ROYAL EXCHANGE                                          626 1120
   EC3

Halcyon Days started in 1950 as an antiques shop which specialized, among other *objets d'art*, in eighteenth-century enamels. Then the owner, Mrs Benjamin, realized that whereas most other eighteenth century *objets*: silver, glass, ceramics and the like had been in continuous production ever since the Georgian period, the enamels made in England at that time had not been produced for over a hundred years. Quite by chance, she encountered a small firm in Bilston (coincidentally one of the original homes of enamelling) who were manufacturing enamel powder for cookers and refrigerators. They had been experimenting in old methods of enamelling on copper and she suggested that they should leave the kitchen and turn their skill to making enamel boxes which she would design. This they eventually did. Today, the partnership is thriving, and Halcyon Days are producing every kind of enamel work; a twentieth-century revival of a popular eighteenth-century art. Parallel to this contemporary side of their business, Halcyon Days are still true to their origins as an antiques shop (they are invited to exhibit each year at the prestigious Grosvenor House Antiques Fair).

There is no shortage of imagination when it comes to Halcyon Days' enamel boxes. Here, there is every shape and size of box, although the proportions and size of their eighteenth-century counterparts can rarely be bettered. Often, the same can be said of the designs. Some are limited editions (again in true eighteenth-century fashion) of reproductions of famous works of art – at the time of writing there is a limited edition of fifty boxes of Sargent's picture of 'Claude Monet painting at the edge of a Wood'. Then there are the commemorative boxes, like the box commissioned by the Marylebone Cricket Club to mark their bicentenary, depicting a match played in 1837. Here too are the 'Museum Boxes', faithful representations of boxes or pieces from the Victoria and Albert, British, Ashmolean, and Fitzwilliam Museums, and two boxes from the Wallace Collection, the designs of which have been taken from a Sèvres dinner service. Also, much sought after, are musical boxes. Typical is a box that plays a passage from *La Bohème*, decorated on the lid with a Zefferelli set from a production at the Metropolitan Opera, New York.

Halcyon Days have also revived the enamel *bonbonnière*, a decorative box originally made for *cachous* to 'sweeten the breath'. These are now made in the shape of fruit, tiny oranges, pears, strawberries, lemons and the like, or little rabbits or birds. Just the right size of *bonbonnière* for artificial sweeteners are their little round boxes with an appropriate message 'Love and scandal are the best sweeteners of tea.'

Whereas the anniversary boxes, 24-carat gold encrusted boxes with a 'round number' on top, and the initial boxes (Quentins, Ursulas, Xerxes and Zoës are out of luck as there are no Q's, U's, X's or Z's) are standard, their other anniversary boxes change every year. There is always a new Easter Egg, a special box for St Valentine's Day, Mother's Day and Christmas Day, and a Year Box, all inscribed with a message and the year.

In that same eighteenth-century tradition, Halcyon Days make enamel boxes to celebrate important occasions. They have made enamels for members of the Royal Family (they have all four Royal Warrants), corporations and regiments, but a large part of their service is for specially commissioned, Bilston enamel boxes, that is 'one-offs'. These boxes are generally entirely decorated by hand and anything can be painted on to the lid: a house, the favourite horse or dog, a coat of arms, a yacht or whatever (the price varies according to the complexity of the subject). It can be done from a good photograph, and allow between three and four months for delivery. Simpler, and cheaper, are the special message boxes, again any shape or size, where the client's own message is put on the lid, outside and in. Allow two to three months for delivery.

Incorporated in some of these boxes is a tiny timepiece. This is another Halcyon Days speciality, as well as eight-day carriage clocks; full size and miniature travelling clocks; pendant watches with quartz movements, all with pretty enamelled designs. Typical of them is their tiny globe of the world which, when opened, has a pretty clock inside. Many, like the Adam or chinoiserie collections, have matching picture frames and boxes.

Also modelled on their eighteenth-century patterns and designs are enamelled candlesticks, *pot-pourri* baskets and *cache-pots*. Halcyon Days always have a fine selection of the originals in stock. Besides these, there are always the best, and probably the largest, selection of antique English enamels to be found outside a museum, as well as such exotica as antique tortoiseshell snuff-boxes, *papier mâché*, *tôle peinte*, Tonbridge Ware, and Regency penwork. All the furniture and pictures in the shop are also for sale.

This is a cosy shop, lit to show off the pieces well, and properly staffed (unlike many London shops, there are always plenty of well-trained assistants, even at the busiest time). Everything can be gift wrapped in their distinctive blue and gold paper. Halcyon Days have a good mail order service. For those who tend to forget an anniversary, St Valentine's Day, Mother's Day or the like, they will send off the appropriate box unasked, but remember to notify them of any changes in your life.

OPEN   Monday to Friday 9.15 am to 5.30 pm, Saturday 9.30 am to 4.30 pm

# Hardy Amies

■ 14 SAVILE ROW                                                734 2436
W1
(*Couture dress designer*)

Hardy Amies chose *Still Here* for the title of his autobiography (written in 1984), a reference to his 40 years as a fashion designer who is 'still going strong'. It was an accurate title too, as Hardy Amies is the only truly old-fashioned haute-couture house left in London, although much of their business is now what they term 'boutique' and ready-to-wear.

There are two collections each year: spring and summer which is shown in January, and the autumn and winter shown in July. There are four customer shows for each collection and though naturally difficult to think of the next season, it is best to order early to avoid the rush in the workrooms later (for couture, allow some weeks and several fittings). Being couture, everything can, of course, be made up in any fabric. Also shown 'on the cat-walk' is Hardy Amies' boutique collection (very limited editions, made in house to a size and then finished off with one fitting on the client), and his ready-to-wear collections. These are mostly made in house (with just a few being bought in), to a stock size, and then altered to fit if necessary at an extra charge. All the Hardy Amies collections cover the whole wardrobe: day and evening dresses, smart suits and coats (at the time of writing, best is the waisted, velvet evening coat with frogging across the front), and blouses. Hardy Amies accessories, like belts, gloves and handbags are all designed with the collections in mind.

While it is obviously better to order from the collection, Hardy Amies can do 'one-offs', wedding dresses being their particular forte. Here the service is even more special: sketches are made until 'everyone is happy', then the usual dress fittings are made until everything is satisfactory. The dress is then delivered to the bride's home, and the fitter will be there on the day, even going to the church (or wherever), to make sure that all is well.

The continued success of Hardy Amies over the years is largely due to his design team. This is now led by Ken Fleetwood (although still very much overseen by Hardy Amies himself). Here, they plan at least two years ahead so that the change in the collections from year to year is never too drastic. For the couture (and for the boutique), they have very experienced saleswomen who are present at all the fittings. Then there is the skill in the workrooms (some of the staff have been there for decades) and, in Hardy Amies' own words, 'double-plus service' that all go to maintain his high reputation.

Here, the Hardy Amies 'look' is paramount: it is an English look, invariably understated and uncluttered, but modern. It is the look of the best-dressed English gentry, many of whom are their clients.

OPEN    Monday to Friday 9.30 am to 5.30 pm

# Hardy Brothers

■ 61 PALL MALL                                              839 5515
  SW1Y 5H2
  (*Fishing rods, reels and accessories*)

When George V was advised to send a telegram congratulating the celebrated novelist Thomas Hardy on his 70th birthday, he sent his royal felicitations to the only Hardy he knew – his rod maker from Alnwick. Hardy rods were the finest then (1910), just as they are now, as hundreds of thousands, Royal and common, have testified.

Today, Hardy rods are mostly made in carbon-fibre (such is their expertise in working with that material, that a whole new carbon-fibre related business has developed making everything from aerials for tanks to violin bows). There are a great number of Hardy rods to choose from, for salmon, trout, and coarse fishing. One of their most popular rods is 'The Smuggler' that comes in three sizes and breaks down into six, seven or eight lengths. Such is the range, there is a particular Hardy rod for every type and size of fish, from a small brook trout in light waters to a large salmon in a fast-flowing Norwegian river like the Vosso.

Carbon-fibre rods are lighter and more durable than the old-fashioned cane rods but, to keep the old skills alive, Hardy's are now making a few split-cane rods. These fine rods, made to a maximum of 9 feet, are all bespoke and so expensive; allow at least six months for delivery.

Hardy's are equally, if not more, famous for their reels (old Hardy reels are collectors' items and command huge prices at auction). Each reel is a mechanical work of art (they have to be as true fishermen are perfectionists) and those features that make them so special have been developed and patented by Hardy's. As with the rods, there is a great variety in each of the seven different reels they make, with a size and mechanism to suit every type of fishing. For the serious big-game fisherman, there is the Zane Grey Reel, a reel produced for and named after the prolific cowboy story writer and fisherman of Hemingway proportions. These are in stainless steel and can be personally engraved.

The Hardy service is special. Minor repairs to rods and reels can be done in Pall Mall; anything more serious is sent to their factory in Alnwick. Hardy Brothers are one of the few who still bother to splice the fly-line to the backing.

Bookings for the Hardy's Casting School are taken at Pall Mall. The school operates from the Highgate ponds in North London, where Andrew Murray teaches beginners (or brushes up the old hands at the start of the season). With a wide knowledge of the fishing available around the country, Hardy's will steer their customers towards a suitable beat or fishing hotel (not recommend for obvious reasons).

There was a time when Hardy's only sold their own products but now, with the demand for the comprehensive range of fishing tackle and country clothing, they sell the best of the rest. They are proud of the fact that all their flies, save one particularly devillish May Fly from Italy, are tied in the United Kingdom. Hardy's have the finest selection of current fishing books, as well as instructional videos (for sale and not for hire). Here, too, is a complete range of fishing (and shooting) clothing, including a 3-ply Gore-tex jacket made to their own design which is 100% water-, wind-, and thorn-proof. Their fishing and cartridge bags, the wax cotton coats, including the Australian Driz-a-Bone, are for country use and wear. However, they do seem to sell many of them as urban fashion accessories and clothes, rather than for their original country purpose (they are not proud at the House of Hardy). In the basement is everything for the coarse- and sea-angler, also the big-game fisherman.

Another of the delights of the House of Hardy is the staff, all fishermen to the man. Their combined knowledge covers every aspect of fishing, game or coarse, sea or big-game. They have just as much time for a duke with salmon rivers in England and Ireland as for a total beginner. So, when fitted out completely by the House of Hardy, from the tip of your rod to the toe of your wader, and you have caught your fish, there is still something else that they can supply: a Cool-fish Bag to take it home. May your lines always be tight.

OPEN   Monday to Friday 9.00 am to 5.00 pm

# Harrods

■ KNIGHTSBRIDGE                                    730 1234
SW1Z 7YX
(*Largest department store in Europe*)

Harrods' motto, *Omnia, Omnibus, Ubique* – all things, for all people, everywhere – is no idle boast. Arguably the world's largest store with 230 separate departments, Harrods is the place where just about everything can be bought – when a friend wanted to give an elephant to President Reagan (when Governor of California, which shows how old the story is), he bought it, where else, but at Harrods? Today, however, the pet shop is tame, with only domestic animals. Harrods has become a landmark in London. It is required visiting for many an overseas visitor, to whom the store, the detail of its edifice picked out in lights, and the house colours of green and gold, are synonymous with the Capital; so much so that these visitors make up over 40% of Harrods' customers.

Although huge, with its eleven entrances and five floors of nearly 20 acres of shopping space, Harrods is not as daunting a place as it appears (for the first-time shopper, it is best to take a free store guide, found at Hans Crescent entrances or the Customer Services Bureau on the fourth floor). In the centre of the store on the ground floor, flanked by the men's department, haberdashery, the franchised cosmetics and perfumes, and jewelry, is the famous Harrods' Food Hall.

81

Here is a gourmet's paradise. As Harrods has a huge turnover in the Food Hall, everything is guaranteed to be absolutely fresh: as they have a huge 'buying power', they can also insist on the very best quality available from their many suppliers. Everything is beautifully laid out too: joints of meat on marble slabs (there is a preservation order on the whole of the Food Hall), the 'sculpture' of fish and sea-food changed daily, the fruit and vegetables displayed with such precision that it seems dreadful to vandalise them by actually buying. Besides such everyday fare as bread (endless varieties), frozen foods and dairy produce, there is more exotic fare such as lobsters, oysters, over 500 cheeses, all game in season, or oven-ready dishes like *poussin* with an apple, venison, quail, walnut, celery and wine stuffing. The health-food shop and groceries are in the basement.

The first floor is given over entirely to women's fashions. Here the floor is laid out in the designer room, with labels from such fashion pundits as Jean Muir, Bellville Sassoon (*see page* 18), Missoni, and the work of other designers, some of whom are represented elsewhere in this book. The second floor is for housewares, which includes bed linen, china, televisions, kitchen equipment and the like, while the third floor has an amazing selection of furniture and all furnishings. The fourth floor is for the younger sets and the sporty, the trendy clothes from 'Way In', every conceivable piece of sports equipment and clothes from 'Olympic Way', and, for the very small, the 'Toy Kingdom'. The fifth floor has the hair and beauty salon, the girls' school uniform and the offices to administer this vast empire.

But Harrods is more, much more, than a department store. Here it provides every possible service for its customers. Apart from such useful services as dry cleaning, shoe repairs, and a pharmacy, there is also a bank, *bureau de change*, jewelry valuation and insurance agency, and a house agency. They will store your furs, and kennel your dog; they will keep your luggage and your valuables safe. They even have a funeral service. Especially useful to tourists, they operate an export bureau and a sight-seeing bus. Theirs is (almost) the last private lending library, with all the latest titles. One great service is their free delivery, in certain areas of London, for account customers and those who pay by credit card.

Harrods is rightly considered the 'flag-ship' of the House of Frazer, and the new owners of the group are no exception. As with all new owners, certain changes are being made, but the essential character of the place, the service and the quality remain as constant as ever.

OPEN   Monday to Saturday 9.00 am to 6.00 pm (Wednesday 9.30 am to 7.00 pm)

# Harvey Nichols

■ KNIGHTSBRIDGE                                              235 5000
  SW1X 1RJ
  (*Exclusive fashion, furniture and furnishings*)

The attractive, and highly imaginative, window displays of
Harvey Nichols are indeed witness to this being the most elegant
department store in London. However, 'fashion house' would
describe Harvey Nichols better, as, not only are four out of the six
floors devoted to fashion, but everything that they sell, be it a
designer dress or a wooden spoon, is 'fashionable'. Part of their
strength is that as they are comparatively small, and so short of
space, their department heads are that much more selective in
their buying, and thus take only the very best. Likewise, the
franchises that operate within the store are of a like mind.

The ground floor is open and inviting, with everything neatly
put together. The best of the cosmetic and perfume houses are
represented, grouped in the centre of the room, and flanked by
such accessories as gloves and handbags, belts and hosiery,
bows and bangles, costume jewelry and shoes, for both men and
women with some well-known names as Rayne (*see page* 138),
Charles Jourdan (*see page* 33) and Church. The menswear is
here with suits from such designers as Armani and Montana,
beach-wear, and the clever sportswear and sweaters from the
franchise of the French Façonnable. Also here under franchise
are Hermès (*see page* 91), Mulberry (*see page* 118), Dunhill
(*see page* 43) and a corner devoted to Cartier (*see page* 28).

The next three floors are given over entirely to fashion
(including the fourth floor which used to house the furnishings
and carpet department). The International Designer Rooms are
on the first floor. Here are the important names in fashion with
their complete range, with designers like Bruce Oldfield (*see
page* 124), Jean Muir, Sonia Rykiel, Jasper Conran (*see page*
104) and Byblos. Harvey Nichols are also particularly good at
spotting, and supporting, talented new designers. Their fashion
buying is complete, in that there is something, be it an evening
dress from the 'special occasions' section, to a bathing costume in
their beachwear section, to suit everyone, whatever their age.
There is plenty of choice, too: their lingerie, for example, has
everything from the sheerest silk slips to thermal underwear. On,
and up, through the next two floors where there is a 'very strong
separates department with important coverage of American and
European collections.'

'Home collectables' is a good description for the goods on the
fourth floor. Harvey Nichols is not a shop for those who need the
basics to start off a home, but for those who need something

special to enhance some part of their house – a special lamp or lighting effect, a piece of glass sculpture or porcelain. Here is the Herend porcelain and the Lalique, with pieces made exclusively for Harvey Nichols, which make such perfect presents, or the delicate pieces of silver, both modern and antique. There is superior stationery and an excellent present wrapping service. What distinguishes Harvey Nichols is that they will go for a complete look with whatever they are selling. For instance, theirs is the American approach for dinner services that really do 'dress' a table; their choice of modern, decorative china, like blue spongeware, really does complement antique pieces. Harvey Nichols also have their own linen, which again covers everything in the linen cupboard. Special to them are their comforters from the United States, a useful bed cover that is half-way between a duvet and an eiderdown. Also on the fourth floor is a promotions corner that changes rapidly, selling fun pieces topical to the moment – St Valentine's day presents, Easter presents and the like. The top floor has a useful restaurant, Harvey's at the Top, the Glemby hair and beauty salon and the toy department.

Suitably sited below ground is Zone (even with a separate entrance), the zany side of Harvey Nichols, with its 'bold shapes, patterns and accessories' with a strong sense of 'tongue in chic'. Again, they mix the established designers with the best of the emergent talent, with concessions like French Connection and Benetton, Virgin Records, with younger make-up from Mary Quant and Bourgois. There is also a Zone Cafe.

To go with all this stylish shopping are many in-house services, particularly for account customers. For them, there is the usual monthly credit and, at sale times (early January and July) a further 10% discount on sale prices. There are also special times for exclusive Christmas shopping, and there is a wedding service for lists. There is an annual store promotion in September (when it is not in April) that features a particular country, colour or season, which percolates through the whole store – from the window displays to the fare served in the restaurant. Client liaison is handled, at the time of writing, by June Ashford, who organizes Harvey Nichols' customers who do not have the time, the expertise or the inclination to shop for themselves, by sending suitable clothes on approval – she even offers a packing service, like a friendly lady-in-waiting, advising what to put in your suitcase for a particular occasion (if it is not in your wardrobe, then she will send it on, be it a safari, a weekend at Windsor, or a yacht in the South Seas). Gail Jones (also at the time of writing) is the colour consultant who, for a modest fee, will tell you what colours suit best and, more important, which colours to avoid.

Harvey Nichols is a pleasant place to shop, with its gentle, almost cosy feel, and quiet service (save for Zone downstairs which is not meant to be quiet or cosy anyway). Up or down, fashion or household, there is a definite Harvey Nichols mark of quality about it all.

OPEN Monday to Saturday 9.30 am to 6.00 pm (Wednesday until 7.00 pm)

# Hatchards

■ 187 PICCADILLY          437 3924
  W1V 9DA              439 9921
  (*Booksellers*)

Hatchards is a proper, old-fashioned bookshop with proper old-fashioned service. It is also an extremely large bookshop with a huge, well-chosen stock that covers every possible subject, except anything too technical. It also has the right feel for a bookshop; smart without being intimidating, erudite without being too scholarly. This is partially due to the enthusiastic staff (so sought after is a job here that Hatchards can pick and choose whom they like). There is also a great sense of tradition here, and so there should be with a firm established in 1797 and still expanding. There is continuity too: it was a terrible shock for regular customers to find that Miss Joy Parker had retired after 20 years on the front counter, but there was just a small compensation to find her there on Saturdays. It is a joy to shop there, and no pun intended on the president and former managing director, Tommy Joy. Bookshop shoppers tend to be rather nice people too.

Fiction, biography and memoirs are to the front of the shop, behind the black, bow-fronted windows (a window in Hatchards is the goal of every author). Here, piled high on a circular table, on a low counter and in deep bookshelves around the walls is the best of those recently published works. Behind, in a large, open room is the non-fiction; tables set up with a particular section, like history and military history by the entrance, a royal table or a humour table further in. Here too are the reference books, business and politics, Bibles and Prayer Books and the like. The next room is devoted entirely to travel and guide books: a feast of world exploration, and slightly tamer stuff, such as the red Michelin guides. The basement is given over entirely to paperbacks, one of the largest stocks in London. Everything is clearly marked in their various sections, and, again, the staff are helpful.

Up the stairs to the first floor where there is every kind of book on art, antiques and collecting, sports, including a large selection of horse books, sailing, skiing and mountaineering, ornithology, with the ubiquitous gardening section (the Royal Horticultural Society was founded on the premises in 1804), cookery and an excellent section on wine. Literature, the performing arts, like opera, the cinema, the theatre, also plays, are on the second floor along with children's books.

The antiquarian book department has been closed down, but Hatchards still operate a search department for customers in that field. They excel in the services that they offer their customers. Apart from antiquarian books, they will find, or try to find, any book, in or out of print, also books from overseas. They have a binding and repair service, and they sell a selection of the 'standard classics' in half and full leather.

A large part of their business is through their mail-order service. There are two catalogues a year, with well over 500 titles and a brief description of each book. They also produce a monthly review slip of around a dozen new books they recommend. Their books go all over the world, a vital link to many. Also typical of their exacting service is to send a client a book or books every month, but only after their preferences have been established. With an encyclopedic memory, they will automatically send their customers works by a particular author, or books in a series, unasked, if they know that they are wanted. Watch out for their signings, just four a year, but always of interest.

Hatchards is an institution. Fortunately for its many thousands of customers worldwide, one that will never fade.

OPEN   Monday to Friday 9.00 am to 5.30 pm (Thursday until 7.00 pm), Saturday until 5.00 pm


# Anouska Hempel

■ 2 POND PLACE                                          589 4191
SW3
(*Women's designer clothes*)

There is little to show from the outside that this is a shop, let alone a *couturière*, and once inside, it is not immediately obvious either. Instead, it has the look, and feel, of some fantasy lady's private sitting room of the *fin de siècle*. Here is total elegance, if not to say opulence. The walls are lined with silk; the curtains that balloon across the windows are nipped back by silken cords and tassels. It is dark (the predominant colours are navy blue, midnight blue and black), but the subdued lighting picks up the sparkle of tall looking-glasses and the sheen of the silk. There are flowers, mostly orchids, everywhere. The furniture is a blend of a Biedermeier sofa and tables, and pieces like the chair with ribbon backs and lamps designed by Anouska Hempel herself and made up by her own craftsmen. A matching pair of pavilions, like some silken Ottoman tent, serve as changing rooms. The main salon is dominated by an early eighteenth-century Florentine carved bed. Scattered haphazardly over the bed is a profusion of hats and dresses as if their owner was preparing for some grand, ducal Saturday to Monday, an Edwardian equivalent to a weekend, and she cannot decide what to have packed. She should, of course, take the lot, for here is everything for that total look of pure elegance and beauty.

Anouska Hempel's approach to creating, and providing, that 'total look' with her designs is thoroughly English, in that her clothes are absolutely right together, without being contrived.

There is that same element of fantasy about them as with her interior decorating: 'If you can swag and drape a four-poster, then you can do it for a body.' The result, especially her clothes for the evening, is particularly arresting and exciting. Here are the ruffles, the bustles and the bows, the full skirts and fuller sleeves, or just a padded band around a dropped waistline, as with one twenties-style dress.

The correlation between her dress designs and her interior decoration goes even further with her use of fabrics. As well as going to the dress-fabric shows for the latest silks, silk taffetas and the like, she will also look out for furnishing materials suitable for her designs, like a particularly rich, brown velvet for a Venetian cloak. She will use the more unusual fabrics too for her evening dresses, such as French ribbon, lace or silk, crushed taffeta. Some of the fabrics, like a rich, ruby red brocade, come from an ecclesiastical shop in the Vatican City. Her day clothes are marginally less flamboyant, but no less romantic for that. Again, some are in the more unusual fabrics of barathea, 'tramlines', a crêpe-de-Chine with raised satin ridges, or *cloqué*, a finely textured silk, even hand smocking.

Anouska Hempel is a perfectionist, and it shows. Everything is made in her own workrooms, and all beautifully finished by hand. Everything that should be lined, like her dresses, coats and suits, is lined in pure silk. Those shoes and hats designed by her, are also made in her own workrooms, although she does import a few hats: the 'padre' and a biretta come straight from the Vatican City.

This shop has great style. The hat-boxes are silk-covered and trimmed with bows; the shoe-boxes are covered in a silk to match the shoes inside. The shoe-trees match too, with the toes filled with dried lavender. The coat-hangers are covered, some with tassels dyed to match and dipped in some exotic fragrance. Even the evening dress hanging-bag, waterproof on the outside, is lined with silk.

While there are always examples of her work ready to wear, Anouska Hempel is mainly couture. Delivery is flexible, depending on the 'rush in the work-rooms', but should not be above six weeks. With such flair, style and quality, Anouska Hempel must be the epitome of luxury shopping in London.

OPEN    Monday to Friday 9.00 am to 6.00 pm

# Herbert Johnson

■ 13 OLD BURLINGTON STREET                    439 7397
   W1X 1LA
   (*Men's and women's hatters*)

'If you want to get ahead', runs the old adage, 'get a hat.' If you want to get a really smart hat, then go to Herbert Johnson, or Herbie J., as they are affectionately known. For around 100 years they have had three distinct sides to their business; hats for men, hats for women and hats for the military. There is also some cross 'pollination' between the departments, like the vogue among some women for the wide-brimmed men's velour hats, or the army officers who invariably go for the felt hats that are as much a part of their uniform as their service dress caps, while all three go for their equestrian headgear.

It would have to be a very strange hat that is not stocked in Herbert Johnson's men's department, for here they sell practically everything to cover the head (where else could you find a velvet smoking cap with a silk tassel, a Clarence cap last seen on an Edwardian bicyclist or a sombrero outside Spain?). However, tradition is very much their line, and the traditional English felt hat is their speciality. This is made from the finest fur felt in a number of distinct styles, some with such military sobriquets as The Sandhurst and Off Parade. Also in durable felt are the waterproof safari and bush hats. The formal hats which are predictably smart, include the homburg, the high-crowned, wide-brimmed Grosvenor, and the bowler hat with the special Herbert Johnson curled brim, and of course top hats, in either black or grey.

Of all their hats, they are probably best known for their tweed hats and caps. The style and tweed of the hats change from time to time, although the basic designs remain constant, *vide* the deerstalker (predictably called Sherlock). A tweed cap is just a tweed cap until you look at those on offer at Herbert Johnson (they are also the only people to make up bespoke caps with their customer's own tweed). Like the hats, the tweeds are constantly changing, but the style remains. Apart from the quality of the workmanship and the tweed, they are readily distinguished from their rivals by the deeper back which makes them more comfortable. There is a variety of styles: the Bond is a full, round cap in heavyweight tweed; the Skye has an eight-piece crown with a button and a press-stud attaching it to the peak; the Crieff is a modern, narrow cap with a sewn-down peak.

For the summer or hot countries, there are the traditional Panama hats (the nearest they get to Panama is the woven-straw, which in fact comes from Ecuador) and the wide-brimmed, cotton Nomad and Riviera. The Panamas and the straw boaters can all be trimmed in bands of your choice (the Brigade of Guards' band is always in stock). For a rainy day, there is always the reversible proofed-cotton rain-hat.

There cannot be much that is smarter in the field than a traditional Herbert Johnson bespoke hunting cap. It has a look of perfection about it, with its high, velvet crown tilted slightly forward. However, sartorial elegance has begun to give way to practicality to conform with the new British Standard Specifications which require a safety harness and are not made to measure. They will still make you a top hat or bowler. Other equestrian headgear includes a jockey's skull-cap, which can be covered with silks or a stretch-velvet cover to simulate a riding hat, and their strong and comfortable polo caps with fittings for a face guard.

All of the hats sold in the shop are carefully fitted and adjusted with the felts steamed to shape. The customer's initials are gold-blocked in the head-band.

The women's department is downstairs in the basement, reached outside from an iron staircase or down the back stairs (just like some of the London clubs where women, if allowed in at all, are relegated to the back stairs). Here they stock a colourful assortment of hats for all occasions. Herbert Johnson are not high-fashion milliners, but create exclusivity for their customers by trimming a hat on the spot, thus giving individuality without the high price.

Alongside all these hats are various other accessories; silk ties, handkerchiefs and umbrellas. They even have their own weather-proof jackets in waxed cotton. There is a colour catalogue, and everything can be ordered by post.

The shop itself has a dependable, quality feel about it with solid mahogany fittings and large, red hat-boxes piled on high shelves. The staff echo the decor; one of the employees was actually trained by the founder, Herbert Johnson, who started the business in 1889.

OPEN   Monday to Friday 9.00 am to 5.30 pm, Saturday 9.30 am to 1.00 pm

# Hermès

■  155 NEW BOND STREET                                499 8856
   W1Y 9PA
   (*leather, women's and men's fashions*)

■  3 ROYAL EXCHANGE                                   626 7794
   EC3

At Hermès, there is far more than a passing reference to their origins as harness-makers in the rue du Faubourg St Honoré in Paris, 150 years ago. Here, the influence and inference of the tack room is strong in practically everything that Hermès produce, in materials (especially leather), in design, in decoration and, above all, in the quality of workmanship. They are at pains to put their clientele first. Their logo of a *duc*, a four-wheeled carriage drawn by a matched pair of horses, that is driven by the owner, is symbolic of their client relationship: where they produce the best, it is their clientele who give it its exclusivity.

Although Hermès still make harness and saddles (at the time of writing they have the last word in hippo-chic, a white saddle and bridle with gold stirrups and bit), today they are best known for their clothes, for both women and men. Again, *le cheval* looms large. Their equitation collection is of the country, and for the country and the *château*: the tweed coats are in a hacking cut, the trousers (this year) are jodhpurs in corduroy or leather. Typical are the hats: very French and jaunty, trimmed with a pheasant's feather. There is even a hint of the stable in their more formal clothes, like the thin band of leather around the classic, grey flannel or whipcord suits, coats and even capes, or some horse motif woven into the silk of an evening suit or dress. The Hermès collections, whatever the season, have that certain elegance that comes with simplicity.

In a more flamboyant mood are their accessories; in particular, the legendary Hermès silk scarf. There are several versions of this each year, each one bright and colourful, 1 metre square with hand-rolled and sewn edges. They are all designed and made in-house, often with a topical theme, and (if it will bear repetition), everything associated with the horse and tack. Whatever the motif, these designs in silk often find their way into other Hermès clothes; the lining for a suit, the turban of an evening suit, the facings of a wool cardigan and the like. The same patterns often appear in their knitwear too. The cashmere scarves are all plain but they come in 22 colours.

The Hermès silks are used in the men's clothes too – in waistcoats, ties, the lining of a suede or leather blouson, or linen travel coats, even braces and dressing gowns. Like their female counterparts, the men's selection of clothes is neat, functional and unadorned. Nevertheless, they are made of exotic fabrics, like the plain, slim-fitting cashmere coats or the silk and cashmere jackets. Then there are cashmere pullovers, cardigan jackets, and silk and cashmere slipovers, even cashmere mufflers. The Hermès 'haberdashery' has lawn handkerchiefs, leather gloves, socks and the like. As famous as the scarves, are the Hermès ties, the designs for which are constantly changing.

The various *parfums d'Hermès*, Equipage, Calèche, Amazone and the new Bel Ami, linger in the air at the front of the shop, while it is the honest smell of leather that pervades the back. Apart from a few saddles and bridles, there is also the Hermès range of luggage. This comes in every size of bag and suitcase and is all made in a black leather with tan edging and saddle-stitched. One bag in the range even has a secret compartment for a jewel-case. Hermès handbags too are famous for design and pure craftsmanship. Typical of their range is the Kelly bag, named after Princess Grace. The leatherwork, which includes dozens of styles of belts and every kind of wallet and pocket book, is made entirely by hand, in Hermès' own workshops.

The same consummate care goes into the design and manu-facture of all the other famous Hermès products. There are Limoges ashtrays, often with similar designs to the silk scarves. These are all hand-painted, therefore anything can be painted to order. There are also exclusive designs on their porcelain dinner services, which include the peony range, and another design of the most exotic toucans. There are still more Hermès delights, such as rugs like horse-blankets with huge checks, or brightly coloured beach towels. There is a new appliquéd bath towel every year (last year the design was a fox's mask).

The tack room comes to the fore again in their jewelry and silverwork. Their museum above the shop in Paris plays a part in the 'new' designs. Here are snaffle bits and curb chains, horse shoes and stirrups, in gold and silver bracelets and cuff-links, necklaces and brooches. There are, of course, other non-hippic styles too. Hermès also have their own watches with round faces and very pretty straps in different leathers; but beware, any Hermès watch sold outside the shop is not made by them.

This is a bright and pleasant shop, with welcoming window displays and an equally welcoming doorman from the Corps of Commissionaires. The interior is soft and restful; the assistants proud of what they sell. Whatever it is that is bought, from a handkerchief to the largest suitcase, it is beautifully wrapped and tied with Hermès ribbon. Quite right too. At Hermès, they are not above tying up the whole shop with their ribbon.

OPEN    Monday to Friday 10.00 am to 6.00 pm, Saturday 10.00 am to 5.00 pm

# Heywood Hill

■  10 CURZON STREET                                       629 0647
W1Y FJ7
(*Superior bookseller, old and new books*)

Heywood Hill is not so much a bookshop but more a literary experience. The shop opened in Curzon Street in 1936 selling books, prints and 'things', but the prints and 'things' have now long since gone. Over the years, they have collected a large number of customers, all of whom trust their judgment implicitly and revel in the very personal service they offer. The staff share out the reading of all the new books, so there is always someone on hand to give an educated view on any volume in the shop (only if asked). Many authors are known to them personally. Add to that their amazing capacity to remember their customers, their customers' likes and dislikes, each member of the customer's family and their friends, *and* all their likes and dislikes too, and you have a unique bookshop. What is even more amazing is that they have never heard of a computer, and most letters are still written in longhand. Thus, when a customer walks into the shop (although they more usually telephone or write, in longhand of course), and asks them to recommend a book, he or she is invariably happy with their choice. Many of their account customers live outside London or overseas and Heywood Hill send them a regular supply of books, a vital link to many. There is also a quarterly list of forthcoming works they recommend. Another part of this service is that they remember if a customer is interested in a particular series, either biographies or novels (say, Anthony Powell's *Dance to the Music of Time*), and will automatically send the next volume when published, unprompted.

With this fine, long-standing relationship with their customers and their needs, Heywood Hill has been able to combine the sale of new books with old and antiquarian books. Very often, they will buy a certain book with a customer in mind. They specialize in books on architecture, flowers, press books and, of course, literature. Unlike any other dealer in old books, they do not have a catalogue (save for just one, produced to mark their fiftieth birthday). Instead, they can find any book in their large stock as if playing Pelmanism.

As their service is so personal and their customers tend to be drawn from the Establishment, Heywood Hill have often been accused of being too grand, imperious and exclusive, an accusation fuelled by their position in Curzon Street, in the heart of Mayfair. This is an unfair reputation, for book-buying if nothing else is entirely democratic, and they take equal care and trouble with everyone who goes to buy.

The shop itself has the appearance and feel of a once-grand London club, but the apparent, outward disorder certainly belies the efficiency within. Books are crammed everywhere, on the round tables in the centre of the room, on the bookshelves that line the walls and piled high in stalagmites on the floor. The new books are to the front of the shop, old books behind and in the

94

basement alongside a good selection of well-chosen children's books.

The staff, headed by one of the directors, John Saumarez Smith, are all kind, helpful and thoroughly steeped in books and literature (at the time of writing, three of their long-standing customers had 'crossed the counter', metaphorically, that is). If you happen on a distinguished, grey-suited figure, kneeling on the floor behind a pile of books taking a long-distance call, cock an ear – he may be recommending your next birthday present.

OPEN    Monday to Friday 9.00 am to 5.30 pm, Saturday 9.00 am to 12.30 pm
No credit cards

# H. R. Higgins (Coffee-man)

■ 79 DUKE STREET                                            629 3913
W1M 6AS                                                      491 8819
(*Coffee*)

The epithet 'coffee-man' as adopted by H. R. Higgins (Coffee-man) Ltd evokes an image of old-fashioned charm, knowledge and service, an image that is not misplaced in their shop in Duke Street. If it is not the window display of large wooden bowls piled high with coffee-beans and a collection of antique coffee-grinders, nor the panelled interior with dozens of copper canisters, brass scales and sacks of unroasted beans, then it is undoubtedly the strong aroma of freshly roasted and ground coffee, which pervades the air, that first entices their customers into the shop.

H. R. Higgins believe in indulging their customers. To them, selling coffee is like selling fine wine. With the knowledge and contacts built up over three generations, they have the reputation of only buying the finest original beans from all parts of the world –they even have the highly prized, and therefore expensive, Jamaican Blue Mountain coffee. Apart from the coffees from Brazil, Colombia, Costa Rica, Mysore, Java and the probable home of coffee, Ethiopia, Higgins has been buying at auction for years a special Tanzanian coffee, called Chagga. With these original coffees and their own special blends there is a coffee for every taste and occasion. Customers may be able to sample any of the coffees before they buy, and all coffee sold in the shop is roasted and, if required, ground on the premises. The chosen coffee is bagged, then beautifully wrapped up in a brown-paper parcel and tied with string.

There is generally a member of the Higgins family somewhere in the shop, Mr H.A., Miss E.A. or 'Master' D. (son, daughter and grandson of the original H.R.), but the staff are also knowledgeable and well versed in the intricacies of selling coffee. They can all place a coffee to suit an individual taste (their current coffee list also has invaluable information and advice). One special feature, also the larger part of their business, is the mailing of regular supplies of coffee to customers all over the world. For this there is a sliding scale of postal charges, but anything over 5lb goes free within the U.K. To go with the coffee and expert advice is a wide selection of coffee-making equipment, from espresso machines to filter papers.

Once you are supplied by H. R. Higgins, you, like their thousands of other customers, are there for life.

OPEN    Monday to Friday 8.45 am to 5.30 pm (Thursday until 6.30 pm, Friday until 6.00 pm), Saturday 10.00 am to 5.00 pm
No credit cards

# Hobbs

■ 29 SOUTH AUDLEY STREET                                    409 1058
W1
(*Exciting provisions*)

There is always a market for the best: the best quality, the best selection, and the best in imagination. Hobbs, in the heart of Mayfair, are certainly of that triple best when it comes to provisions and certain wines and spirits. They are not so much concerned with comparatives, but with superlatives (why else would the majority of top London chefs patronize them?). Every single item in the shop has been chosen with care. Everything with the distinctive Hobbs label has either been specially prepared for them by proven suppliers (many items have been imported directly from abroad), or prepared by Hobbs themselves, to their own, secret recipes. Their reputation for fine, exotic food has been created by their founder, Romilly Hobbs, traveller, gourmet and specialist in European cuisine.

Hobbs are indeed special when it comes to choice, having the best of the best. Take caviar. Here they have not only beluga (and the cheaper Sevruga), but also the vodka to go with it. But it is no ordinary vodka. Besides the standard Stolichnaya, they have their bison vodka, Zubrovka, a lemon vodka, Limonnaya, and a chili pepper one, Pertsovka. Another speciality is gravadlax, raw, marinated salmon, which is traditionally eaten with aquavit, the Swedish spirit. For some strange reason, the best aquavit has crossed the Equator. Naturally, the aquavit sold by Hobbs has crossed the Line.

The more ordinary grocery items are equally available and special at Hobbs. A tea biscuit is a tea biscuit until presented with the Hobbs selection: a butter biscuit, a ginger biscuit, a hazelnut biscuit, a cinnamon biscuit, all thin and very good. Or their tea: here there are just three teas, Earl Grey, Assam and Darjeeling, blended to their own taste, loose or in tea-bags; nothing special except that the tea-bags are of muslin and hand-filled in India. There are also a few herbal teas from France. The selection of jams stretches even the most vivid imagination, with such treats as gooseberry jam with orange and walnuts, medlar jam from Italy, blueberry jam, plum jam with port, and three-fruit marmalade. Their lemon curd is delicious, and, for those with the taste for it, so are their peanut butter and cashew butter, prepared without salt.

The choice is no less limited for oils and mustard. The olive oil is, naturally, the finest from the first pressing, while the choice of nut oils is wide: walnut, grape seed, sesame seed, almond, and the like. There are over twenty different mustards, both English and French, to choose from, including one as unlikely (but good) as garlic and parsley. Their horseradish, like their chutneys, is famous. The choice of vinegars, over twenty, is no less exhausting, with the likes of champagne, thyme, raspberry and *herbes de Provence*.

Predictably, the selection of cheese is exotic with proper Mozzarella made from buffalo milk from Italy, fine goat cheeses from France and baby Stiltons. The eggs are brown and free range. The fruit and vegetables are fresh and luxurious: fresh figs and mangoes, limes and Cape gooseberries, star fruit and peppers, whatever is in, and out, of season (there are potatoes too, but these are first earlies, small, and beautifully matched).

Hobbs have their own house champagne as well as that of the better champagne houses. Their wine list is small and, although adequate, appears to be there for the convenience of the food shopper rather than in its own right.

Prepared in their own kitchens is an impressive selection of *charcuterie*, *pâtés*, terrines, salads, cold meats and the like. Here too are the prepared dishes, like stuffed tomatoes, the *oeuf en jelée*, and the filo pastry filled with chicken and pine nuts. There is also an outside catering service.

An enviable present must be a Hobbs hamper, especially at Christmas. These come in seven stock sizes, in either red or green baskets, and can be made up specially to order. The stock hampers are filled with such treats as a dozen bottles of champagne (from house champagne to Cristal), to a side of smoked salmon. These are delivered free within central London (if the order is over £50), or are sent by carrier. As befitting such a shop, the predominant decor is of a rich burgundy colour. The staff are fittingly dressed in black waistcoats and aprons. Superfluous to say, there is the most delicious, inviting aroma about the place. Those on a diet, enter at your peril.

OPEN    Monday to Saturday 10.00 am to 7.00 pm (happy hour, when perishable goods are sold at half price, 6.00 pm to 7.00 pm)

Hobbs and Co. have incorporated: John Baily and Sons (*see page* 14)

# Holland and Holland

■ 33 BRUTON STREET                                    499 4411
  W1X 8JS
  (*Gun-maker, all shooting accessories, presents*)

During Holland and Holland's centenary celebrations in 1935, the rival gun-makers, James Purdey (*see page* 135), said of them, 'You as a firm stand for the very best and finest points in the British gun trade.' That was over 50 years ago, and today Holland and Holland still stand for that same excellence, high quality and

98

service in each of the three sides to their business – gun-maker, shooting school, and shooting accessories and clothing.

They claim that some of their customers know about guns, but the majority of their clients go to Holland and Holland as their staff know about guns. It was Queen Victoria who gave Holland and Holland permission to use the sobriquet 'Royal' as a trademark for their best quality, double-barrelled guns and double-barrelled rifles. Today, they are still making these fine 'Royals', the shot guns with their special Holland and Holland self-opening actions, in every bore for which cartridges are available (.410, 28, 20, 16 or 12 bore), and the double-barrelled big-game rifles in most proprietary calibres. To order these bespoke guns or rifles, the specifications are first discussed in the Gunroom in their Bruton Street shop, then the client's exact measurements are taken at their shooting grounds in West London. Samples of finely grained walnut for the stocks are produced, or, if time allows, the choice can be made from a larger selection at their factory in North London. A particular feature of any gun from Holland and Holland is the high standard of embellishment; standard 'Royals' have their own distinctive Royal scroll. Clients can have any engraving they wish, either from Holland and Holland's own book of engravings, or from a photograph, print, or engraving, even designs made up with coloured, precious metal inlays. It will be anything up to three years before the guns are ready, and in that time, many hours of 'exquisite skill' go into their making. The guns come complete with case, slips, and tools. Also 'bespoke' are their cased, presentation revolvers.

Besides the Holland and Holland Royals, they also produce their own boxlock gun, the Cavalier and the Cavalier de luxe with its walnut stock, fully engraved to the client's specification. Their magazine rifles, used all over the world, are made in all the calibres of the well-known American and European cartridges. Here, too, is a large selection of the better makes of second-hand shot guns and rifles, as well as antique and black powder weapons. They undertake repairs in their factory, and give insurance valuations for insurance purposes in the shop.

Part and parcel of the shop is the shooting school in north west London at Duck's Hill Road, Northwood, Middlesex HA6 2SS (telephone: 65-274 25349) where everyone is catered for, from a rank beginner to the senior shot at the start of the season.

But the sale of guns is only a part of Holland and Holland's business, for at their Bruton Street shop they also supply everything that could possibly be connected with shooting: from a sheepskin lined gunslip to an extra-large pigskin cartridge bag; from a cased gun-cleaning tool box to a dog whistle. They can supply every known type of cartridge, however obscure.

The shooting clothing department is large and comprehensive, both for the practically and for the sartorially minded. They have everything for foul weather and fair: waxed cotton coats and jackets, loden and quilted clothing, smart shooting suits, knickerbockers and plus-twos as well as safari clothing. Holland and Holland have recently taken over Rowland Ward, who, although no longer taxidermists, do have a fine range of gifts, notably engraved glass, hand-painted china, especially Herend, all with a strong sporting motif. There are sporting paintings for sale too.

Their book department specializing in Field Sports is comprehensive, for both contemporary works and those out of print, and a few antiquarian books. The titles are all catalogued in an up-to-date booklist (available on request). They also operate a book 'wants' service. There is also a selection of videos on shooting.

Holland and Holland is staffed by a team of helpful experts. The shop is just what you would expect, a cross between a rather grand gunroom and the hall of a sporting country house. Big game trophies line the panelled walls, the odd suit of armour graces a corner, and the parquet floor is covered with a Persian rug. If a butler were to come out and offer you a glass of sherry as you spoke to your new-found shooting 'friends', it would not seem at all out of place.

OPEN    Monday to Friday 9.00 am to 5.30 pm

# H. Huntsman and Sons

■ 11 SAVILE ROW                                            734 7441
W1X 2PS
(*Bespoke tailor*)

Huntsman are proud of the fact that, alongside the care, quality and attention to every suit they 'build', just as much hand-work is involved today as there was 60 years ago. They are also proud of their reputation as one of the finest tailors in Savile Row (and that, without being partisan, means the world), so much so that nothing can leave their premises unless *they* are totally satisfied with it.

There are no short cuts to a Huntsman suit. The customer is met by the salesman and the suit discussed. They will, of course, make anything the customer wants, but it would be rather a waste not to go for the Huntsman style. Here there is nothing elaborate, no extraneous pockets, no exaggerated shoulders. Instead, they go for a pleasing line – the coat close fitting at the chest, waisted, then slightly flared like a hacking jacket. As there is no such thing as 'the perfect body', so the *perfect* fit to the normal body would look a little odd. Hence their skill is needed for creating that 'perfect line' to compensate for these failings.

Then the cloth is chosen. Naturally, only the best is on offer (this is also in their own interest as inferior cloth is more difficult to work). Huntsman not only have the full range of English cloths from the mills, but also many special to them. They have their own tweeds and a few heavy worsteds – some as much as 18- or 19-oz cloths which are coming back into fashion (these 'perform' better, look better and last even longer).

The customer is then measured by the coat fitter for the coat, and the trouser fitter for the trousers, who then cut their respective patterns. Everything is done in house by tailors on a salary, not on piece work, which means that nothing is skimped, everything is checked for quality. The suit is then put together for the first, or baste, fitting (dictionary definition: to sew together lightly). They are then taken apart, however well they fitted, or rebasted if not satisfactory. Then there is the forward fitting (at this the facings and pockets are in, the sleeves tacked in, as is the lining). If this is not right, then the procedure is repeated and another fitting arranged. The suit is still not complete even at the finished-fitting stage, with the button holes, cuffs and the like, to be finished by hand – unlike their competitors who make an envelope at the cuff, Huntsman sew their cuffs so that they are flat.

Although they get their name from their founder, a Mr Huntsman, and not through their association with the hunting field, they do make hunt coats and riding jackets, but not breeches (there is even a wooden horse and saddle in every fitting room). Huntsman tailor for women too, but only the more classic suits – no doubt the kind that Bertie Wooster's Aunt Dahlia wore. Huntsman are now much into ready-to-wear suits and coats, and at half the price of a bespoke number, they are extremely good value. There is also a shirtmaker on the premises. Various accessories – socks, ties, sweaters and the like – are also there for convenience. The shop is exactly as you would expect: no frills but solid. There are the mahogany tables and cupboards, piled high with bolts of cloth (mostly their own worsteds and tweeds), Persian rugs on a parquet floor, and an open fire. The staff have been there for years. They claim you feel 10 per cent better with a Huntsman suit: there are many who would put the percentage higher.

OPEN    Monday to Friday 9.00 am to 5.45 pm (closed for lunch between 1.00 and 2.00 pm). Closed for the first three weeks of August.

# The Irish Linen Company

■ 35/36 BURLINGTON ARCADE           493 8949
   W1V 9AD
   (*All linen*)

Anyone who has slipped in between a pair of smooth, linen sheets, and rested their head upon a linen pillow case, will never wish to sleep on anything else ever again, despite the initial cost and the supposed difficulties of laundering them. As a fabric, linen is exceptionally hard-wearing (being hygroscopic it is the only fibre that is stronger wet than dry). Linen sheets are beautifully cool and crisp in hot weather, and always fresh, whatever the climate. The Irish still produce the finest linen in the world and the best is bought by the Irish Linen Company in London – there was a time when Co. Down was one of the most highly industrialized counties in Great Britain, with countless factories manufacturing pure linen. Today, there are only a handful of mills left.

There is plenty of choice in all things linen (and in superior cotton) at the Irish Linen Company. Sheets come in all sizes, from a small single to the largest king-size bed. The decoration on the linen is either standard embroidery-work (done by outworkers in Madeira or China) or specially embroidered with monograms, coronets or any motif of your choice. Some sheets and pillow cases are sent to Belgium to be trimmed with lace, like the handkerchiefs that go to Paris to be trimmed with Alençon lace.

The Irish Linen Company also specialize in the finest linen double-damask table-cloths and napkins. Since they are so closely involved with the weaving of their linen damask, they pride themselves on being able to produce the near impossible. Their damask is woven wider than most, which means that they can accommodate enormous sizes – if you have 24 to dine (allow for generous elbow room), they can supply a table-cloth to order measuring 7 feet 6 inches by 21 feet – in that case it might be a case of cutting your table to suit your cloth. Nor will your guests be stinted on table napkins. The Irish Linen Company have a number of sizes including a 24 inch square, as well as 22-inch and 18-inch squares. They will also embroider initials, cyphers and coronets onto their table-cloths and napkins.

There are heavily embroidered table-cloths too. Again, these are finely worked in Madeira and China and come in all sizes and colours (the company had to admit defeat just once when they could not supply a full-length 14 foot 8 inch circular cloth made out of a single piece of damask). Not everything here is vast. They sell fine linen huckaback towels, handkerchiefs, luncheon sets (eight place mats, napkins and a centre runner), even linen glass cloths and the ultra-fine percale cotton sheets and pillowcases.

Part of the success of the Irish Linen Company is that it is the only privately owned shop left in London selling linen. It is run by Martin Addleman, the third generation in the family business. He is assisted by an able staff who know their flax. They send their linen all over the world, as they have done since their founding in 1875.

OPEN    Monday to Friday 9.00 am to 5.30 pm, Saturday 9.00 am to 4.00 pm

# ▌The Italian Paper Shop

■ 11 BROMPTON ARCADE                                    589 1668
   SW3
   (*Marbled paper and desk accessories*)

Who would have thought that a shop devoted to selling Italian hand-made marbled papers, however beautiful, would be a success in London? Obviously Tim and Emma Hanbury did when they saw them in Florence and they were proved right.

Tucked away in the Brompton Arcade, the Italian Paper Shop sells these exquisite papers in about 50 designs, each one 'hand-decorated according to the procedure of Marie Ruette, book-binder to Louis XIII' – in the seventeenth century. There are a few cheaper Italian papers for present wrapping but they are a mere pastiche of the real thing.

The rest of the shop is taken up with everything that could possibly be covered in marbled paper. Most of these are useful items made pretty or pretty things made useful. The former are all items that are used in the office – box files, letter racks, pencils and pencil-boxes, waste-paper baskets – while the latter are things like book-ends and obelisks. There is a good selection of photograph albums and little books with plain paper for recording beautiful thoughts (keep them short as the books are often too small to be of any use!). Apart from the marbled objects, they do a splendid line in genuine Florentine masks and postcards that you would be happy to send.

As you would expect, the shop is attractively laid out with a courteous manageress.

OPEN   Monday to Friday 10.00 am to 6.00 pm, Saturday 9.30 am to 5.30 pm

# Jasper Conran

■ 37 BEAUCHAMP PLACE                                    589 4243
   SW3
   (*Women and men's designer fashions*)

Jasper Conran's first shop is very much a designer shop. Voted Designer of the Year in 1986 by the British Fashion Council, his designer clothes are set in the shop designed by Nigel Coates, each one complementing the other. Like Jasper Conran's clothes, there are no frills to the shop; bleached oak floorboards and shelves, simple black rails and light fittings, soft photographs, proper-sized changing-rooms with lights and mirrors and bowls of lilies.

Since bringing out his first independent collection in 1978, Jasper Conran has been steadily expanding that collection, for both women and men, for the complete wardrobe (collections that now include cruisewear and lingerie). Where Jasper Conran is particularly successful is in the breadth of his collections. Everything is carefully co-ordinated, whether designed by him or specially for him, as with some of the accessories, like the marvellous range of colours of the cashmere scarves, shoes, jewelry, even hats.

In true Conran style, everything is beautifully wrapped (with tissue paper printed with a map of London showing the shop), and parcelled in red, blue or green carrier bags and tied with ribbon. A fitting departure.

OPEN   Monday to Friday 10.00 am to 6.00 pm (Wednesday until 6.30 pm), Saturday 11.00 am to 6.00 pm

# Kanga

■ 8 BEAUCHAMP PLACE                                       581 1185
  SW3 1NQ                                                 589 3784
  (*Specialized dresses*)                                 225 1611

Like kangaroos (diminutive form, Kanga), Lady Tryon, owner of this shop, comes from Australia. Lady Tryon (nickname, in some quarters, Kanga), produces and sells bright and pretty dresses in her own shop in Beauchamp Place. While these day and evening dresses with their exotic colours echo an English summer's day, they also bring a little Australian sunshine to a grey and drab winter's day. They are extremely versatile, not to say practical, and very feminine.

Kanga dresses have many advantages, not least that they all come in just one size and fit all but the most diminutive. They have the distinction that they suit all ages, and can be worn anywhere. Dressed up or dressed down, they are right for almost any occasion, from dropping the children off for school in the morning, to a day in the Royal Enclosure at Ascot, or for a drinks party in the evening. Being uncrushable, they are also perfect for travelling; they are washable and drip-dry as well. Likewise, the long evening dresses are as right for an informal dinner as a grand dance.

Apart from the fact that these dresses are unique and thus totally different, the secret of their success is that they are made of polyester georgette. This georgette comes from Japan, the only place where they can print the fabulous colours properly, and are made up in Hong Kong, regretfully the only place where they understand the fabric. Although the basic concept remains the same, London-based Lady Tryon's own designs and choice of colour change annually with the seasons.

What more could one ask of a single dress?

OPEN   Monday to Saturday 10.00 am to 6.00 pm (Wednesday until 7.00 pm)

# Karl Lagerfeld

■ 173 NEW BOND STREET                                    493 6277
  W1
  (*Women's designer fashions*)

Karl Lagerfeld, a German living in Paris, is one of the most prolific, and versatile, designers today. He is prolific in that, as an innovator, he is fashion leader; versatile, in that he designs for both his own label and for, and in the style of, Chanel (*see page 30*). His clothes are designed very much as a single collection, to be worn together, in their own right, rather than mixed with anything from another of his (or indeed anybody else's) collections, 'otherwise you mess up the proportions.' On the other hand, as his clothes are so unique, they tend not to date.

Lagerfeld's clothes are undeniably chic, with a definite Lagerfeld feel about them. He is possibly best known for his evening wear, like his beaded evening dresses, but he equally well designs 'from head to foot, day or night.' There is great attention to detail – the line of a pocket, the cut of the shoulder, or just some simple adornment.

The shop, on two floors, is pure art deco, geometric with greys and blacks, and provides a good backdrop to the Lagerfeld collection.

OPEN    Monday to Saturday 9.30 am to 6.00 pm (Thursday until 7.00 pm)

# Robert Lewis

■ 19 ST JAMES'S STREET                                   930 3787
  SW1A 1ES
  (*Cigar merchants*)

With a cigar, condition is all important: a moderate cigar in good condition is infinitely better than a top brand-name cigar in poor condition. At Robert Lewis you obtain the best of both worlds with the widest possible selection of the best cigars, all in perfect condition. And so they should be, this being a family firm and the oldest cigar merchants in London (established 1787).

The original Robert Lewis began by selling snuff and they still stock enough varieties for their clients – those whose jobs preclude smoking, like churchmen, judges, gas-fitters and the like. However, after Wellington's troops returned from the Peninsular War with 'tobacco wrapped in a leaf', cigars became popular and the Robert Lewis of the day fostered a new fashion in smoking. There is no question that the best cigars today are still Cuban. Although the whole cigar operation is now nationalized, Robert Lewis still have their contacts and suppliers in Cuba built up over eight generations, which ensures a continuity of quality and supply. These Cuban cigars are all the finest, hand-made cigars from cigar houses such as Romeo y Julieta, Montechristo, El Ray del Mundo, H. Upmann and Partagas. Lewis's also have their own brands (imported Cuban leaf and rolled in England) called, predictably, St James's, the other is Solamente. They also stock cigars from other countries: Honduras, the Dominican Republic and Mexico (especially for the U.S. market where Cuban cigars are not allowed), Jamaica, Sumatra, the Philippines and Burma.

All these cigars, as well as their customers' cigars, are stored and matured under controlled conditions in the basement of the shop. Lewis's cater for both the English taste for dry storage and the Americans' preference for wet.

Besides these cigars, Robert Lewis sell a few exotic cigarettes, like the Turkish Balkan Sobranie and Sullivan and Powell (who also do a Virginia cigarette). They have their own mixtures of pipe-tobacco and will also make up a special blend to suit a client. They sell pipes, exclusive to them – 'Nothing special,' they claim, 'except that they are the best.' Everything conceivably connected with cigar smoking is available, from a simple box of matches to a sophisticated humidor. The helpful and knowledgeable staff are headed by the jovial proprietor, Mr Croley. The shop has just the feel and ambiance about it that you would expect -- parquet floors, panelled walls, glass-fronted cabinets and that pleasing smell of fresh tobacco.

OPEN  Monday to Friday 9.00 am to 5.30 pm, Saturday 9.00 am to 12.30 pm

# David Linley

■ 1 NEW KING'S ROAD                    736 6886
SW6 4SB
(*Bespoke furniture*)

David Linley has teamed up with Matthew Rice to make exceptional furniture. It is a fruitful partnership, for David Linley, who trained at Parnham House, knows about making furniture, while Matthew Rice studied theatre design at the Central School of Art, and so has the advantage of not having a training in furniture making. Thus, when a piece of marquetry furniture (very much their forte), is proposed and designed by Rice, he is not limited by the constraints of what can, and what cannot, be reasonably created with inlay. Although Linley has the skill to make each piece himself, they are, in fact, given to other craftsmen who make everything, by hand.

The first collection of David Linley Furniture was based on a series of Matthew Rice's watercolours of Venice. This theme, with its bold and interesting Venetian architectural features and strong colours, translated particularly well into marquetry. Part of the success of that initial theme was that it works well, be it a large screen, a desk, a bookcase, a table, or even the small frame of a looking glass. There is a limited edition of 25 of any one piece of furniture in a collection, and each one is signed and numbered. Although there are quite often 'Venetian' pieces or the like at their shop in the New King's Road, most of their creations are for special commissions from both private clients and from the more imaginative interior designers.

At David Linley Furniture, they relish a challenge. They will make anything, from the smallest pencil box (only here what they made was an exquisite pen cabinet) or a chess/backgammon table, to a full set of chairs or a 48-foot board-room table, even a piano. As each commission is different, the finished piece is the result of a close interpretation of the client's wishes combined with their particular skills. In the tradition of the great eighteenth-century furniture makers, the final design is submitted to the client in a watercolour on the heaviest of cartridge papers. Once agreed, it is then translated into the various veneers and woods, each one chosen for its colour and texture. They mostly use sycamore as the base because it takes a stain well, or, being white, it is a good contrast to the coloured inlays, like ebony and rosewood, ash and oak, magnolia and Swiss pear, and many more. Because of their size, and hence scope for the designer, their folding screens and doors are extremely successful. Again they work on a theme, like a Bahamian scene for a house in Lyford Cay, or a view of London for the Berkeley Hotel.

Their pieces, of course, do not have to be inlaid or follow a particular theme; the client's wishes are paramount. Some of their work is contemporary, like David Linley's own black folding desks, chairs, Canterburies and screens.

An extension of their Venetian theme is everything for the desk-top in paper. There are blotters and pen holders, waste-paper baskets, envelope and paper holders, with new additions in the same theme every year. There is also another set based on medieval tiles from the British Museum.

David Linley Furniture is unique. Here they promise something special; they deliver just their finely worked furniture, that is exactly right, wherever.

OPEN Any time by appointment. Weekdays from sometime shortly after 9.00 am to around 6.00 pm, Saturday mornings – best to telephone first

# J. Lobb

■ 9 ST JAMES'S STREET                    930 3664/3665
SW1A 1EF
(*Bespoke boot- and shoe-maker*)

Mr Lobb has been making boots and shoes for over 125 years; same name, same family, and the same high quality of workmanship and service, and, for a good many of those years, many of the same styles.

To have a pair of shoes made here is an experience, although judging by their ever-full order books and delivery time of over six months, their many thousands of customers over the years call it a necessity. The two glass-fronted cabinets on one wall are filled with examples of their shoe-styles – brogues and Oxfords, brown and whites for Goodwood races and the summer, evening-dress shoes and Derbys, Monks (with a strap) and Norwegians (with vertical uppers). Special to Lobb's are their slippers that are usually made up in velvet (with gold initials, a coronet or whatever), but quite often in the customer's own worked *petit point*. They make every kind of boot too, an elegant, short jodhpur, a tall hunting or polo boot, even a Newmarket boot. As styles change so rapidly in women's shoes, they generally settle for a standard court shoe, a golfing brogue or the like. If a sample shoe is not there, then 'If it can be described, Lobb's can make it'. Once the style has been chosen, the fitter will measure the foot; the clicker then chooses the skin or hide and cuts out the uppers. They use dozens of different skins and hides of every weight and colour, from a fine box calf to a heavy grain hide, with every type of leather from antelope and doe-skin to ostrich, crocodile, Morocco or lizard, even the ears and trunks of elephant. Then the last-maker makes the last, the closer sews the uppers, and the maker puts on the sole.

Lobbs recommend that these fine hand-made shoes have their own wooden shoe-trees. When the shoes need repair, they prefer that they be returned to them so that they can be put back on the last to get back into shape, rather like a pedal gymnasium. Lobb's have their own special shoe polish, and liquid (and bones) for waxed calf. They can also supply special shoe cabinets to order, and bespoke shoe trunks and cases.

What is fascinating about this place is that most of the shoe is made on the premises, with the last-maker actually working to the side of the shop. The smell of leather is strong; the sense of history stronger (they have the Duke of Wellington's boot on display). There is almost a hallowed feel about the place, slightly dark with deep leather chairs and caring fitters. An experience or a necessity? Whichever it is, a pair of Lobb's shoes or boots will be worth it, on both counts.

OPEN    Monday to Friday 9.00 am to 5.30 pm, Saturday 9.00 to 1.00 pm
No credit cards


# James Lock

■ 6 ST JAMES'S STREET                                    930 5849/8874
SW1A 1EF
(*Hatter*)

Surveying the new reformed Parliament of 1832, the Duke of Wellington declared that he had 'never seen so many damned bad hats in m'life'. He was speaking not only metaphorically,

since many of the new members had top hats not made by Mr Lock, a fact of which he strongly disapproved. Today, Mr Lock (although he is called Richard Stephenson) is still making hats and selling them from virtually the same premises, as has been done for over 300 years.

Fashion, by dint of being fashion, is constantly changing, and no more so than with the current trend of men's hats. One's loss is another's gain: where few wear a hat in the town, they have taken to them in a big way for the country. However, at Lock's, they cater for both, with all types of hats.

Of their many styles over the years, Lock's are most famous for their Bowler hats – only here they are called Cokes, after William Coke who commissioned the first one (Bowler was the man who made it). Here they keep all sizes of Cokes which can be fitted to the exact shape of the customer's head. For this, they use a *conformateur* which measures and re-creates the head exactly, so that the hat can be moulded, within a few minutes, for a perfect fit. The same method is used for hunt caps (their styles are called The Quorn and The Pytchley), which means that they should not come off in a fall. However, these do not conform to the British Standards Institute as there are no unsightly straps about the chin. They do sell BSI approved hunt caps, but, because of the padding, these cannot be fitted. Lock's top hats, for morning dress and hunting, are also fitted by the same method, but are no longer silk (the judicious use of stout to the felt with a sponge will make it indistinguishable from the real thing). Also in the hard-hat range are polo caps, with five colours to choose from, although they can be made up in any team colours. Inexplicably, Lock's have a huge demand for solar topees and 'helmets-pith, one'. Semi-hard is the Homburg in black, brown, two greys and navy blue.

The nomenclature of the soft hats is all roughly indicative of their purpose. The Executive, the Chelsea and the Madison have the ring of the City about them, the Sandown, Wetherby, Lingfield, Kempton and the Goodwood Panama are racing numbers, while the Sloane is a wide-brim velour hat (dark blue, black, grey, green, brown and red) and is much favoured by women as well. These are all steamed to shape. The Derwent and the Ghillie sound like fishing hats, although the Regent and the Connaught appear to be named after the tweed, rather than any Royal connections. There is a Links cap and shooting caps; particularly stylish is their Cowal (as worn by this author), an eight-piece tweed cap. For the coldest winters there are the fur hats in muskrat (which is not a rat), wolf, fox, beaver and astrakhan.

This is a shop full of interest and history. Famous antique hats adorn the windows; hat boxes are piled high on shelves and the uncarpeted floorboards give the place a seventeenth-century feel. The staff has changed gradually over the years, although some have been here since 'top hats were six guineas, hunting ones were eight'. If a hat does not look right on a customer, the staff will be totally honest and say so. After all, they have seen 'so many good hats' in their time.

OPEN     Monday to Friday 9.00 am to 5.00 pm, Saturday 9.30 am to 12.30 pm

# Paul Longmire

■  12 BURY STREET                                930 8720
   ST JAMES'S
   SW1
   (*Jewelry, especially cuff-links*)

Paul Longmire's shop has the air of a rather grand library of a country house; even the doorway, with its Royal Warrants above the pediment, is somewhat reminiscent of a glazed front of a Georgian bookcase. Apart from the beautifully arranged windows, there is only a hint inside that it is primarily a jeweler's shop, as both rooms, upstairs and down, are furnished with fine English and French furniture, pictures and pretty *objets d'art*, all of which are for sale.

Apart from building up a reputation for finding special pieces of antique jewelry and rare objects for clients, Paul Longmire also specializes in cuff-links or, as they are sometimes known, sleeve-links. At any time there are over 500 pairs in stock, with varying price-tags. Some are old (not antique, as cuff-links are only a late nineteenth-century invention); the rest are modern, made to their own and Edwardian designs. They also create individual cuff-links for their clients in their own workshops, not least the presentation sets for most members of the Royal Family. Although they pride themselves on being able to make up anything, the usual request is for a straight-forward enamelled four-plate cuff-link on silver, silver gilt or gold (9 or 18 carats, 14 carats for the U.S.A.). They cater for everyone. Where they do decorate cuff-links for institutions and organizations, universities and regiments with their relevant colours and crests, it is with the more personal cuff-links that their originality is apparent.

For them, nothing is too much trouble, in fact they welcome a challenge. They have committed their clients' houses and cars, horses and dogs, and children (in that order) in enamel to cuff-links, all from a colour photograph. They also have reflected their clients' sporting interests (and aspirations) in cuff-links, like their polo-team colours with crossed polo sticks; yachting with the club and/or their personal burgee; golf club colours and crossed clubs, and, most popular of all, racing colours (the silk vest on one plate, the jockey's cap on the other). To be certain of those specialized colours, it is best to come armed with a photograph of the jockey wearing the silks and cap, and a snippet of the actual material. Failing that, a good crayon drawing will suffice.

Enamelled or engraved armorial cuff-links, badges or pendants are another Longmire speciality, either crests or coats of arms, and, for the Scots, a crest and clan tartan. They have many of the relevant heraldic directories, including Fairburns with 165,000 entries for all over the world. Everything can, of course, be engraved straight on to the gold or silver plate, or produced in reverse crystal. Depending on the time of year, delivery for commissioned work is normally between three and four months.

The owner, Paul Longmire, is generally in his shop, but in his absence, his staff are also knowledgeable and helpful.

OPEN    Monday to Friday 9.00 am to 5.00 pm, or by special arrangement

# Manolo Blahnik

■ 49–51 OLD CHURCH STREET                    352 8622/3863
SW3 5BS
(*Italian hand-made shoes*)

This shop, in a quiet street off the King's Road, is pure Manolo Blahnik. Everything, save the eighteenth-century sofa and a painted, Maltese table, has been created by him. The rest of the furniture, the chairs, sofa and shelves in a delicate ironwork with a strong Etruscan flavour, were made to his design: his decor, with its rubbed out, painted walls, reminiscent of a house in Pompeii, has now been copied so often by interior decorators that it is to be changed. The window and shop display have been arranged by him. The flowers are white. The shop has a charm of its own, borne out of its innate elegance and pretty things. But it is for his beautiful shoes that Manolo Blahnik is most famous.

Manolo Blahnik designs and makes shoes for both women and

men. His shoes are virtually couture, there being never more than 12 pairs (often as few as eight), of any one colour, in any one style. There are, however, 50 to 60 styles in each of the two, annual collections. As that dozen pairs of shoes covers all sizes (from 34 to 42: English size 2 to 8: U.S. 3- to 9-), it is best to be there at the launch of the new collection – mid-February for the summer collection, the end of August for the winter collection. Occasionally, one or two summer shoes appear before Christmas to whet the appetite.

What puts Manolo Blahnik's shoes in a class of their own is his very individual style, the materials he uses, and the quality of workmanship. The shoes are completely hand-made in Italy. He uses a variety of materials: the best silk satins, grosgrain silk, wool (at the time of writing, black-and-white hound's tooth), linen for the summer, plain and exotic leathers, like lizard and baby crocodile. A Blahnik shoe is instantly recognizable, either for its pure, classic line or for its embellishment – one typical feature is an exaggerated tongue that can be twisted into any shape to alter the appearance of the shoe. Special too are his wedding shoes (usually in stock) of woven silk satin in off-white and cream; and also his flat pumps, in silk satin covered with sangaal lace.

As well as shoes, Manolo Blahnik makes boots, either in suede or leather: long like a riding boot, and short (at the time of writing) like a court jester's boot. Again, these can adapted to alter the height and style. Every boot and shoe has a name, such as Brigitte Bardot for the tall suede boot and Ampelia for the flat pump.

There are just a few shoes for men, like their evening pumps with a silk bow, some stylish lace-up shoes, boots and slippers, some in an exotic cow skin.

This is very much a family business, and it shows. The beautifully shod sales assistants (led by Manolo's sister, Evangeline) have the gift of treating each customer as if she or he were the only one who mattered. And rightly so, for their customers swear that their shoes are as much a pleasure to buy as to wear.

OPEN    Monday to Friday 10.00 am to 6.00 pm, Saturday 10.30 am to 5.30 pm


# Henry Maxwell

■ 11 SAVILE ROW                                          734 9714
W1X 2PS
(*Boot- and shoe-makers*)

The name of Maxwell has been synonymous with hunting boots since the turn of the century, just as it was synonymous with the box-spurs that the original Maxwell invented in the 1750s. Although a pair of hunting boots is now out of reach for all but the discerning rich, Maxwell's still make affordable shoes and slippers.

A Maxwell boot is very smart and easily recognized with its straight back and concave front. They are made so that when the wearer is mounted, the calf is pushed out sideways giving the boot an extra-slim line when viewed from the side. As a pair of top hunting boots or polo boots takes from three to four months to make, it is advisable to order them in the summer or winter respectively. After the initial measurement (in the right weight of sock), it is wise not to take up jogging as that exaggerates the calf muscles – the reason our fathers' and grandfathers' boots rarely fit the modern leg is that they rarely walked anywhere, far less ran, and so had the narrowest of legs. When you arrive to collect your boots, beautifully boned, 'treed' and bagged, they will last, if cared for, a lifetime, or at least a very long time indeed.

While Maxwell's standard styles of shoes cannot be classed as high fashion, they are what nanny would call 'sensible' shoes, and thoroughly practical and very English. Within their range are brogues, golfing shoes, robust walking shoes and Norwegian (with straight sides). Maxwell will, of course, make up anything to order and relish the challenge. Clients choose a style from samples in a glass case and the leather from a wide selection. Their foot is then measured and any foot abnormality carefully recorded (again wear the right weight sock). The last for that style of shoe is then made by one man, the uppers cut and stitched by another, but both on the premises. Uppers and last then go to the shoemaker, who traditionally works at home. The lasts are kept for anything between 30 to 50 years. Shoes can be made up in three to four weeks but they are better if they can be made more slowly. They should always be returned to Maxwell for repair where they are reworked on the original lasts.

Slippers and pumps are also a Maxwell speciality, which also gives the client a greater scope for originality. They will make them up in virtually anything – velvet, tapestry, even polychrome bead-work supplied by one client. They will embroider anything, from plain initials and coronets to signs of the Zodiac and bees – and, for one client, a waxed moustache.

Henry Maxwell and Co are situated in the basement of their parent company's shop, H. Huntsman and Sons (*see* page 100), the last Maxwell leaving the firm in 1972. The shop is exactly what you would expect of an old-established firm, being comfortable and unpretentious. The staff are all polite without being obsequious, and decidedly knowledgeable.

A pair of shoes or boots from Henry Maxwell and Co is

undeniably expensive, but then if you divide the price by their expected life, they become cheaper than ready-mades. If not convinced by that argument, then try 'You never regret an extravagance.'

OPEN   Monday to Friday 9.00 am to 5.45 pm (closed 1.00 pm to 2.00 pm)

# Monty Don

■ 58 BEAUCHAMP PLACE                                       584 3034
   SW3 1NZ
   (*Costume jewelry*)

This is a *bijou* of a shop. The walls are a deep-red Chinese lacquer, set with bevelled mirror panels; the furniture and showcases, made specially for the shop, are black. Sparkling against this rich background are Monty Don's collections of costume jewelry.

This jewelry succeeds at two levels: the classical and the witty, as both are beautifully designed, and extremely well made. Monty Don's pieces are all cut from lead crystal, like a diamond (which accounts for that added sparkle), and are hand-set. Other pieces are in sterling silver. The traditional pieces, including necklaces and large brooches, have an Edwardian opulence about them, while the fun pieces, like the fish's skeleton, cairn terrier earrings and brooch, and crabs are jokey, without being silly.

Costume jewelry is here to stay. After all, it is not enough now to be wearing a pair of little gold hoop earrings in the evening to be dressed up.

OPEN   Monday to Friday 10.00 am to 6.00 pm, Saturday 10.30 am to 6.00 pm

# Mostly Smoked

■ 47 ELIZABETH STREET                                     730 8367/8368
   SW1W 9PP
   (*Smoked food*)

Although it cannot have taken much imagination to dream up the name Mostly Smoked for this shop, they do have some pretty imaginative smoked foods for sale here. However, amongst their more unusual products, it is for their smoked salmon, the most available of all smoked foods, that they are most renowned.

All the smoked salmon from Mostly Smoked is wild salmon from Scotland. It can be bought either fresh or vacuum packed, as a whole side ('sliced and laid back', or un-sliced), in 1-lb or ½-lb packs. They also do ½-lb packets of gravadlax, a Swedish invention of raw, marinated salmon. Also, customers can have their own fish smoked ('fish' being the purist game-fisherman's term for a salmon), or indeed any lesser fish. Besides salmon, Mostly Smoked have a splendid ichthyological range from a variety of the best British smoke-houses: smoked trout, eel, buckling, tuna, mackerel, herring, haddock and kipper with shellfish like smoked scallops, mussels, and prawns. The smoked cod's roe is particularly good.

Their smoked game and poultry is no less exotic. Apart from the humble chicken made mighty by the skill of the smoker, Mostly Smoked have smoked poussin, quail, turkey, duck, pheasant, pigeon, even goose from Israel. Meats, too, come under the smoke with loin of pork, venison and, of course, ham. Their bacon and sausages are special.

Nothing appears to escape the smoker. Good, English hard cheeses, like Cheddar and Cheshire smoke particularly well, also the more unusual cheeses like Mozzarella. Who would have thought of smoking frogs' legs, quails' eggs, or hickory almonds? They are all there at Mostly Smoked, as is everything to go with these smoked products – chutneys, port and the like.

Mostly Smoked Christmas Hampers are proper hampers, in that they are useful picnic hampers (as opposed to a useless, chi-chi basket that some other shops pass off as a hamper). The standard selections are delineated by price, or anything can be made up from their range to order. Delivery is free within the London area at all times, and charged at cost outside.

The shop is clean and clinical, but the white tiles are enlivened by their logo of a leaping salmon, or 'fish' in piscatorial terms.

OPEN    Monday to Friday 9.00 am to 6.00 pm, Saturday 9.00 am to 1.30 pm

# The Mulberry Company

■ 11–12 GEES COURT                                           493 2546
ST CHRISTOPHER'S PLACE
W1
(*Leatherwork, especially suitcases, country clothes*)

118

The Mulberry Company thrives on its very Englishness – it is after all a very English company, from the heart of the West Country. It makes traditional English leatherwork and now clothes, with English hides and fabrics. But being English is not enough on its own, especially in the competitive world of fashion and accessories. The quality of their workmanship, the choice, excellence and originality of their materials, and their design set them apart.

Belts were the making of the Mulberry Company. The styles were, and are, greatly influenced by the saddler and harness-maker's trades. Typical are the plaited leather belts exactly like plaited reins, or plain leather with heavy stitching down the sides and around the buckle. Today, there are over 100 styles of belt to choose from. The saddler's influence is also strong with hand-stitched bags of every description: handbags (modelled on cartridge, shooting- and fishing-bags), dispatch bags, pigskin brief cases and attaché cases. There is a great variety of texture in the leather of all bags, most of which, like the crocodile, lizard and snakeskin, are printed onto calf.

From there, it is a short step to luggage. Here Mulberry use a simulated leather called Scotchgrain which is tough and durable, waterproof too, and trimmed with harness leather. The range of zip-up bags is comprehensive, including their International Grip, the largest size an airline will allow as hand luggage. These come in six colours: navy, black, khaki, chestnut, ice and mole.

Characteristic of the Mulberry Collection is their Planner, in every kind of leather. This is that much larger than the standard organized system (too large for some, so they have produced a smaller version). With the Planner, there is, of course, the widest selection of papers to go in it. Mulberry Company tortoiseshell sunglasses do have a certain chic.

The clothes for the country really are country clothes. Their shoes are bench-made and tough, their waxed-cotton coats well thought out and attractive. The riding coat really does have poppers down the back to go over the horse's back; and the flaps over the seams of the long drover's coat do keep out the wet (there is even an instruction leaflet on how to look after the coat, and a tin of waterproofing wax). There is no attempt at fashion at the Mulberry Company although there is that little something that makes their things special – such as a leather collar on a wool shirt or a coat.

The shop itself is, of course, rural with stripped pine and polished boards, creating a good foil for their eclectic stock. However, whatever they sell they can guarantee its provenance; after all, it is carrying their logo of a Mulberry Tree.

OPEN    Monday to Saturday 10.00 am to 6.00 pm (Tuesday until 7.00 pm)

# Naturally British

■ 13 NEW ROW
COVENT GARDEN
WC2 4LF

240 0551

(*Hand-made crafts, country clothes and presents*)

This is a shop you either love or loathe, depending on your taste for craft and 'things'. As its name implies, the goods here are thoroughly traditional, worthy, British and hand-made; so much so that they almost carry guarantees that they contain 'no artificial colouring or preservatives'.

The strength of the shop is its very Britishness, particularly for the overseas visitors. Elgar grinds away in the background; nothing is stamped 'Made in Taiwan'. Even the shop-front, double-fronted bow-windows painted the green of a stand of English oaks in summer, looks as if it has been transferred from a Hogarth print. Inside Welsh dressers, Victorian display cabinets, tables and shelves are crammed with their wares (from over 300 separate suppliers), like an old-fashioned nanny's sitting room. There are cabinets with silver, glass, and bits of jewelry, stands of walking sticks with animal heads in bronze; soft and wooden toys (best are the jig-saw 'sculptures' by Monkey Puzzle). To the back of the shop are clothes, mostly Fair Isle and hand-knitted sweaters, and carpet bags (made, supposedly, from the unworn surrounds of Persian rugs) and attractive reproduction eighteenth-century cheval and table mirrors. Downstairs is an ethnic dream with pottery, mostly Rye, Norfolk and Dartington, and wooden 'things' for the kitchen (chosen possibly more with an eye for decoration than practicality). There are baskets of pot-pourri and baskets for logs. Kitchen clocks 'go well'.

The shop was conceived, and is owned and run by Jon Blake, assisted by an efficient staff (such is the unemployment situation today that he can choose them from any number of tri-lingual graduates). Where everything in the shop is for sale, much of his business consists of special orders and the 'personalizing' of various of their goods. Of the former, their old-fashioned rocking horse is the best – it is said that the reason the privileged British ride well is that they all started on rocking horses in the nursery. Personal, hand-carved public house signs may not be to everyone's taste, but the enamel boxes, glass and finely bound books made up to their customers' own design could be of greater interest. Dog baskets too can be made in Norfolk reed given the dog size; St Bernards are a speciality.

OPEN  Monday to Saturday 10.30 am to 7.00 pm

# New and Lingwood

■ 53 JERMYN STREET                                    493 9621/5340
SW1Y 6LX
(*Shirts and shoes, ready-to-wear and bespoke*)

It was obviously a good match when Miss New went into partnership with Mr Lingwood in 1865, for, not only did they found what is judged as one of the finest shirtmakers in the country, but they also married. Both liaisons began in Eton, the former to the benefit of the College, the latter doubtless for their mutual benefit. Today, the Eton connection remains one that has lasted for more than five generations in the same family. Although the firm catches its customers young at school (or later when up at Cambridge where it has another shop), New and Lingwood's main branch is in Jermyn Street, on the corner of the Piccadilly Arcade.

New and Lingwood shirts are instantly recognizable. They have their own collar shape and are double-cuffed. They are also full-bodied and the tails long for comfort and for a ready supply of material when those collars and cuffs fray. For town wear, besides the plain colours, there are, amazingly, six different stripes (a Bengal stripe, fine Bengal, and standard, also ladder stripe, fine stripe and fine fine stripe), all made up in 100 per cent cotton poplin. For the country, there is a selection of Oxford

121

check shirts in cotton or flannel (button cuff). Dress shirts are either silk or voile. They are also one of the few stockists of band shirts for stiff collars. All the shirts are made in their own workrooms. Many of their customers still have bespoke shirts (for new customers, they insist on a minimum order of three shirts). The patterns, and samples of the materials in stock, are kept in the basement and, depending on the season, the shirts take between six and eight weeks to make. They are firm favourites with army officers for whom they make fine, khaki shirts.

Alongside the shelves of shirts are other New and Lingwood luxuries: dressing gowns in lambswool, chenille and silk pyjamas, ready-made or bespoke in poplin. There are scarves and sweaters (even 8-ply cashmere) and socks, especially bird's-eye and Argyle styles, some coming in a cashmere and nylon mix. There are hundreds of silk ties in every hue and colour. Who would have thought that there could be so many variations for a spotted dark blue or deep red tie?

Upstairs are the shoes, which, like the shirts, are either ready-made or bespoke. The term 'ready-made' certainly belies the quality of these, as they are all bench-made on lasts, and all hand-finished. They are made to New and Lingwood's own inimitable styles, with many variations to choose from, like the town shoes (black or brown) in brogues and half brogues, Oxfords or the elastic-sided Cambridge; shoes with buckles and shoes in horse hide. There are casual shoes (some with tassels, some in reversed calf), and country shoes, like the waterproof Veldtschoen Norwegian shoe or the brown Derby much favoured by army officers, as are their reverse-calf chukka boots. For the Scots, or those of Scottish origin, there is the lace-up ghillie shoe. True to the classical associations of Eton is the corduroy Grecian slipper, also on hand are the black velvet Albert slippers with a variety of decorations. Their bespoke shoes are a thing of rare beauty, with a great variety of styles and all of the finest calf, kid, crocodile, lizard or buckskin leathers. All shoes from New and Lingwood should be returned to them for repair.

Although very expensive, a tan, leather-hide attaché-case will last a lifetime. The full range of leather luggage, both pure hide and green waterproofed canvas with leather trim, is also built to last, and to withstand even the worst baggage handlers.

At New and Lingwood, with their continued Eton connections, the carpet is Eton blue, even the Sellotape is in the Eton colours. A portrait of one of their original hatters, Solomon, ironing an Eton top hat hangs over the stairs. It is a place where individual and polite service prevails (led by their merchandising director, John Carnera) although the staff baulk at the wearing of stiff white collars, whatever the weather.

OPEN    Monday to Friday 9 am to 5.30 pm, Saturday 10 am to 3 pm

122

# Tommy Nutter

■ 18/19 SAVILE ROW            734 0831
W1
(*Stylish bespoke tailor*)

One of the joys of patronizing Tommy Nutter is that you never know with whom you will be rubbing those distinctive Nutter-style shoulders – Barbra Streisand, Elton John, even a trendy peer of the realm. Before designing and building suits, Tommy Nutter studied draughtsmanship and building techniques with the then Ministry of Works. He learned his tailoring craft as a boy trimmer in an old-fashioned firm, before rising on the high tide of swinging London in the Sixties and dressing every pop and film star. Unlike the majority of those customers, Nutter survived and is still flourishing.

Today, he has considerably toned down his extravagant ideas, both for his bespoke suits and ready-to-wear collections – his is tradition with a twist. That said, his current style is still instantly recognizable. The shoulders are square, the jacket close hipped and without a vent. The trousers are baggy, high-cut and have turn-ups, and always buttons for braces. The waistcoat is either matching or in another material such as moiré silk or brocade. The cloth is traditional and British – the finest flannel, Huddersfield fine worsted, classic checks, Prince of Wales checks and chalk-stripe. Pure cashmere is the ultimate in suiting material. For shooting suits, he uses Scottish and Donegal tweeds. He also has a good line in dinner jackets. They are mostly three-piece and double-breasted with ribbed-satin lapels, silk basket-weave buttons and horseshoe waist-coats. He also does the semi-stiff shirt and silk bow tie to go with it. The tail coats are traditional as 'you cannot muck about' with them.

Tommy Nutter will design anything for those who want something different. He begins with a sketch (ask him nicely and he will give it to you at the end) and, when agreed, the suit is then made on the premises. It takes around two months to complete with three fittings. His clients are nearly all men. A Nutter suit is good value, being 'more expensive than some but not nearly as much as others'. Bespoke shirts are also made there; David Lobb, bespoke shoemaker, calls every Thursday to see his customers.

On the ready-to-wear side, he has a fine range of suits, exciting knitwear, shirts and trousers. Ties, particularly double-ended bow-ties, are another speciality. Tommy Nutter clothes are seen around and are very popular. With a Tommy Nutter suit, just think what company you are in.

OPEN    Monday to Saturday 9.00 am to 6.00 pm

# Bruce Oldfield

■ 27 BEAUCHAMP PLACE                                    584 1363
  SW3 1NJ
  (*Women's designer fashions*)

Bruce Oldfield has that great talent of being able to design women's clothes so that the wearer not only looks good, but she also feels good in them. While his clothes are extremely feminine, it is the line he creates with the imaginative use of fabric that sets him apart as a designer. Bruce Oldfield really understands his fabrics, and knows what can be done with them; how to drape and curve matt jersey and silks, how to fashion wools, linens and gabardines, creating natural folds last seen on an ancient Greek sculpture.

But it is for his cocktail and evening dresses that Bruce Oldfield is renowned, and at his most exciting. Here he can display his art with such fabrics as silken *lamé*, checked taffeta, satin, *cloqué*, even frothy net. He will mix fabric with fur; one rich, evening dress in velvet is trimmed with mink; another, an embroidered evening jacket, is lined with mink and shows a mink collar. For day, with his suits, dresses, blouson jackets, skirts and jackets, Bruce Oldfield is no less adventurous, with a strong, tailored look. Again, he creates his distinctive line through the cutting and the use of his fabrics and suedes. Everything is made in his own workrooms, where they claim that 'the finish is exact, the fine trimmings denote the attention to detail of a couture-based designer.'

Bruce Oldfield is both couture and ready-to-wear. As with the other designer houses, there are two ready-to-wear collections a year. With the two annual couture collections, a few examples are made up, the rest being left as sketches, from which orders are taken. The chosen garment is first made in muslin, the *toile* fitting, followed by at least three more fittings; wedding dresses, an Oldfield speciality, take at least four fittings, 'brides invariably put on or take off weight before their wedding day.' He will also do 'one-offs', but his couture is so specialized that they, too, are virtual one-offs.

There is a range of Bruce Oldfield accessories, belts, patterned hosiery for Charnos, and shoes for Rayne (*see page* 138).

The shop in Beauchamp Place is simple, rather than imaginative (that is left to the clothes themselves). The staff are all true *vendeuses*; experienced and honest in their opinions. They are, after all, selling something that goes far beyond a dress.

OPEN   Monday to Friday 10.00 am to 6.00 pm (Wednesday until 6.30 pm), Saturday 11.00 am to 5.30 pm

# Paul Smith

■ 43–44 FLORAL STREET            379 7133
COVENT GARDEN
WC2E 9DJ
(*Men's designer clothes*)

■ 23 AVERY ROW            493 1287
W1X 9HB

There is a view that it is just as silly to make clothes that are so expensive that no one can afford them, as it is to design clothes that no one can wear. Not so on either count for Paul Smith, designer of a whole range of men's clothes. His is a 'no-nonsense approach to fashion, and provides a consistently inventive, and exciting, line in modern classics for men'.

Paul Smith will mirror the tailors of Savile Row in his suits and coats, but will include those barely perceptible touches of design (such as, the curve or the width of the lapel) that make his clothes special to him. The choice of fabric is original too, often made up specially for a particular style of suit he has in mind – a light overcheck on a plain worsted stripe, a fine doeskin (what Naval Officers' uniforms were made of), and the traditional tweeds. Often there is a witty twist, even an eccentric flavour, to Paul Smith's clothes as with some of his sweaters or specially printed cotton for shirts. His clothes are well made (usually with British fabric and certainly in Britain) with great attention to detail.

Paul Smith is also strong on design, design with a capital D. With a critical eye and magpie instinct, he fills the rest of the shop with things that appeal to him, anything from Swiss Army pen-knives to Kettland coffee percolators, and lengths of Kente cloth from Ghana to a collection of Alessi plates.

This is an exciting shop, with a young and friendly staff. The shop fittings are antique from a Sheffield former chemist. Paul Smith's work is far better known abroad than in his native England. The customers are there because they know about him by reputation, editorial or word of mouth. Truly, 'No prophet is honoured in his own country'.

OPEN    Monday to Friday 10.00 am to 6.00 pm (Thursday until 7.00 pm), Saturday 10.00 am to 6.30 pm

# Paxton and Whitfield

■ 93 JERMYN STREET     930 0250/0259/9892
 SW1Y 6JE
 (*Cheese*)

'Even when out hunting, Mr Jorrocks' thoughts were never far from his dinner, and the cheese Paxton and Whitfield supplied him with.' Established in 1797, Paxton and Whitfield had as great a reputation then for supplying the best cheeses (including that for Surtees' Mr Jorrocks in 1834), as they have today; no doubt the cheese Jorrocks mistook for the moon after dinner came from Paxton's too.

Besides being the oldest cheese shop in London, Paxton and Whitfield also have the widest selection of cheeses in the capital. Here, there are over 300 of the finest European cheeses, of which anything between 40 and 50 are English (or at least British). With each variety it is the 'farmhouse version' that is chosen, since it has a truer taste and is slightly stronger in flavour than its supermarket-bland equivalent. Each new type of cheese, whatever its provenance, is personally chosen by the buyer (Paxton's is still a family-run company), generally from its traditional home –the Stiltons from Leicestershire, the Cheddars from Exeter and so on. Paxton's also keep up with all the new cheeses, like the new British goats' milk cheese and the ewes' milk cheese.

General de Gaulle once remarked on the difficulty of running a country which had 365 different cheeses. Since many French cheeses are similar in taste and texture (as are other European cheeses), Paxton's have concentrated on one good example of each. So, among the many varieties of Brie, voted by some the 'king of cheeses', they have chosen the Brie de Meaux, with its strong, rich flavour made from unpasteurized milk. There are unusual cheeses too, like the ewes' milk cheese from the Pyrenees called Prince de Claverolle, a Dutch Gouda flavoured with stinging nettles, or from Tiverton, Devon, an English goats' milk cheese called Vulscombe.

Paxton's clients are diverse, in that they range from the connoisseur and the keen amateur, who wants to know more about cheese, to those who just want something different. Paxton's have their share of browsers too, as there is always a sample cheese or two cut up to try, or a promotion from a region or country.

The customers are well served by the staff, all of whom are trained, and know about the cheeses they sell. They have the time, and inclination, to help (their nearest equivalent must be a good bookseller). Customers are invited to taste a sliver of cheese before they buy something new, so should never be disappointed.

There is everything that goes with these splendid cheeses too: the biscuits (wheat and sweet), the chutneys, the mustards, the sauces and relishes, and the wines (in a limited range). There are pâtés from Belgium, and traditional English, chicken-and-ham and game pies. Their Yorkshire hams and Wiltshire bacons are famous. Their teas have been whittled down to a dozen of the best original blends, like, for example, the White China Point which is pure China tea.

Paxton's have a Christmas hamper which, like everything else (except soft cheese in summer), they deliver in London, or send by first class post. The shop, with its splendid Georgian front, is little changed inside since Edwardian times, save that there is a glass counter dividing the cheeses from prying fingers. How Mr Jorrocks would enjoy it all!

OPEN   Monday to Friday 8.30 am to 6.00 pm, Saturday 9.00 am to 4.00 pm

# N. Peal

■ 37/38 and 54 BURLINGTON ARCADE            493 5378/9220
W1V 9AE
(*All cashmere, women and men*)

It takes the soft, under-hair combed from twenty-four Mongolian goats (or a few token goats from Kashmir) to make one cashmere coat; the product of three goats for a man's sweater, two for a woman's jersey, and just one for a scarf, and that is just the beginning of many, many intricate processes that metamorphose that hair into a sweater, or whatever. Having the largest selection of knitted cashmeres in the country, N. Peal sell the product of hundreds of thousands of goats from their functional, rather than pretty, shops in Burlington Arcade (they operate a thriving, world-wide, mail order service as well).

N. Peal are *the* specialists in cashmere; it is, after all, all that they sell. Here are the women's classic cashmere sweaters, in every colour, hue and style, that have been favourites for years (not least the ubiquitous twin-set). Here too are what they term the 'updated classics', the old classic sweaters adapted by their own in-house designers to bring them in line with the current fashion. When it comes to fashion in cashmere, those same in-house designers lead the field. Typical are their double-breasted jackets or the shawl-collared sweaters, or the roll-collar sweater

127

that goes so well with the long-line cardigan. There are special cashmeres for the evening, embroidered with birds or the like, or emblazoned with diamanté. Then there is the round-necked tunic with a detachable cowl (this also doubles as a roll-neck, even a cummerbund). Also particularly chic are their cashmere capes, some (to order) trimmed with dyed fox-fur or mink.

The men are no less well catered for with all the classic cashmere sweaters, V and round neck, in dozens of colours, ribbed or cable. There are the Argyle sweaters (with the diamond pattern) and those with intarsia fronts, where the pattern has been inlaid by hand. There is every weight of cashmere sweater from the thinnest, sleeveless slip-over or polo shirt to a magical 10-ply. Besides the multitude of sweaters, there are the cardigans (including a shawl cardigan called 'The President', as worn by John F. Kennedy), and reversible blousons, even smoking jackets. There is also an impressive array of cashmere socks (most mixed with 25% nylon for strength), some plain, some Argyle, some bird's-eye.

For its weight, cashmere is the warmest fibre in the world. N. Peal have a fine selection of scarves (some lined with Paisley silk), gloves and wonderful rugs and blankets. Their cashmere dressing gowns are surely the height of luxury. However, the ultimate must be the cashmere track suit. Whatever would that Mongolian goat think of that?

OPEN   Monday to Saturday 9.00 am to 5.30 pm (Saturday until 4.30 pm)


# The Pen Shop

■ 27 BURLINGTON ARCADE                              493 9021
   W1
   (*All types of pens*)

Before the days of the ball-point and the felt-tip pens, fountain pens were a necessity. Today, that necessity has almost become a luxury, one that is often classed as a designer object or a mere accessory. However, for the stylographists, there is a haven in stylish Burlington Arcade at the Pen Shop. Here, they sell all the leading brands of pens; the makes that are not only aesthetically pleasing to look at, but are also pleasing to use.

There is little to choose between the top names in print from all over the world (except Taiwan). There is the established Mont Blanc from France, as are Yves St Laurent and Dupont; the

American Sheaffer and Cross; the Lamy, Elysée and the precise Pelikan from Germany. The good old English firms are represented by Parker, Dunhill and the 'Yard o' Lead' (Waterman, thought of as English, is in fact French). Then there are the Swiss Caran d'Ache and the Italian Aurora. The gold (or silver) pens and pen sets, like the ultimate hand-crafted Samouelle, that used to be obligatory presents have now been largely superseded by the Chinese lacquer 'designer' pens and the like.

This is a slip of a shop. It is presided over by the owner, Mrs Hunt, a kindly person who takes the same care and trouble with each customer, whether they spend a fortune on pens or buy a box of leads for a propelling pencil. Pens can, of course, be tried before purchase (have something planned to write on the pad so as not to emulate the endless squiggles and illegible signatures). Although the pen itself cannot be changed, they will change the nib within ten days if not suitable. It seems that there is a bottomless basement for they carry a comprehensive stock and all accessories to go with their pens like ink, cartridges, refills, leather pen cases, and so on. Pens bought there can be serviced and repaired; they can also be monogrammed. Often, antique ink-wells are on sale as well. With a proper pen from the Pen Shop, just think of all those beautiful thoughts that will flow from the nib.

OPEN   Monday to Friday 9.30 am to 5.30 pm, Saturday 9.30 am to 5.30 pm

# Penhaligon's

■ 41 WELLINGTON STREET                          836 2150
   WC2E 7BN
   (*Fragrances and all toiletries*)

■ 55 BURLINGTON ARCADE                          629 1416
   W1

■ 4 KNIGHT'S ARCADE                             584 0137
   SW1

■ 20a BROOK STREET                              493 0002
   W1

■ 69 MOORGATE                                   606 5355
   EC2

London is rich in shops that seem absolutely right: the right decor, the right ambiance, the right position, and, of course, absolutely the right product. Penhaligon's, perfumer, in Covent Garden is just such a shop. Here are the traditional Victorian fragrances, sold from what appears to be a contemporary shop, in a Dickensian part of London. From the moment you push open the glass-panelled door and the spring-bell stops ringing, you regress to the age of the founder, William Penhaligon. He set up his original business in Jermyn Street, next to the Hamman Turkish Baths. Penhaligon's colours of burgundy and gold reflect the rich flavour of the shop, the dark oak panelling, the mahogany cabinets and chemists' drawers, and the jars of essence. The only part of Penhaligon's that does not match the Victorian image is the staff, who, although dressed in the house burgundy, are bright and jolly.

If any original customers were to buy something from Penhaligon's today, they would find that little has changed. The same, natural and traditional recipes of the Cornish founder are still used today; the same ribbon is hand-tied round the neck of the bottles, even the labels are indistinguishable from the original. Only the bottles are marginally changed in that they are now metric and the stoppers fit better.

True to his origins as a barber, Penhaligon created five distinct fragrances for men. There are the appropriately named Hammam Bouquet, a suitably exotic blend of rose, jasmin, and English lavender and a hint of sandalwood created for the Turkish Baths; Lords made of lemon, bergamot and sandalwood; Blenheim Bouquet and English Fern (used by ladies and gentlemen alike). These all come in various preparations, *eau de toilette*, colognes, after shave and shaving balms, soaps and shaving soaps (in wooden bowls), bath oils and deodorants, some with talcum powders. Then there are their *eau de colognes*, extract of limes and two hair dressings, Aleimma and Bayolea. There is everything to go with these toiletries – badger shaving brushes, cut-throat and safety razors, brushes and combs.

For the women, Penhaligon's fragrances are naturally more feminine, with such bouquets as Jubilee (revived for the Queen's Silver Jubilee) of French moss, oakwood and sandalwood; Victorian Posy, a fresh blend of wild rose, winter jasmin and lily of the valley, while Bluebell is 'cool and woody'. These all come in *eau de toilettes*, skin balms, bath oils, soaps and the like. Their floral toilet waters are a positive all-year garden with Elizabethan Rose, Gardenia, Lily of the Valley, Orange Blossom and Violetta.

There is everything here too for the dressing table: Victorian scent bottles like the silver-topped globe bottles, enamelled topped jars and bottles, brushes, antique silver backed and modern, also swans'-down powder puffs. Often they have antique dressing cases, complete with all the bottles, and the modern equivalent in leather which they call the Duke of Wellington Campaign Bag. There are hand-mirrors and silver frames, soap-dishes and antique jars of all sizes. Another pretty Victorian antique which is always in stock is the comforter – a glass phial with silver caps, one end for smelling salts, the other for scent. Everything can, of course, be filled with anything appropriate.

For the new customer, there are testers to sample the various fragrances. Penhaligon's wrapping is akin to gift wrapping, for everything is wrapped in burgundy. The wrapping changes for Christmas to gold printed with a Victorian Santa Claus and child. Delivery is by their vintage van, also in burgundy. This is the very place to find more than just a whiff of the past; you can even pass it on with a scented postcard.

OPEN   Monday to Friday 10.00 am to 6.00 pm, Saturday 10.00 am to 5.00 pm

# Polo Ralph Lauren

■ 143 NEW BOND STREET                                     491 4967
W1Y 9FD
(*American designer clothes for women and men*)

'He lived in an exalted world. A world of clipped accents and hedges, of fine people and cars and houses. Everything seemed perfectly in place. I longed to push open the iron gates, knock on the great door and enter . . .'. This is just the imagery that Ralph Lauren has tried to re-create in the clothes he designs (not to mention the decor of his shops as well). It is pure Gatsby and Brideshead 50 years on.

Three distinct ranges (largely delineated by price) make up the overall concept. At the top end, there are the collections designed by Ralph Lauren and shown twice yearly. Here are the expensive fabrics, the silks and the cashmeres, the satins, the velvets and the finest linens. Next comes their 'classics' line, which is a distillation of the designer collection at a quarter of the price. Lastly, there is what is termed 'rough wear', the jeans and the denims, the heavyweight sweaters and rugged suede for the country and, perish the word, leisure.

Whichever bracket a particular garment falls into, it still has that unmistakable Polo Ralph Lauren look about it (very often it

131

carries his logo of a polo-player). Another mark about his clothes is that they are all extremely well made, with an extravagant attention to detail. Ralph Lauren's clothes do not date. There is an enduring quality about them – the more casual even improve with age when faded and frayed.

There is nothing (save for glitzy evening dresses) that is neglected in the women's extensive range. Although they are clothes that have been 'designed', they are not 'fashion'. Instead, Ralph Lauren takes a classic design and re-interprets it in his own way with colour, cut and fabric. Typical is his herringbone tweed coat with a velvet collar, and a cape with matching trousers in Prince of Wales check. He is an innovator too: who would have thought five years ago of mixing a satin blouse with a tweed jacket or a velvet jacket for daytime?

The men's formal clothes are very clubbable; wear them in Whites or the Knickerbocker. Typical are the chalk-stripe suits, the double-breasted pheasant-eye suits, dinner jackets and the covert coats with velvet collars. Accompanying them is a solid range of shirts, some styles very traditionally American with button-down collars. Typical too, are the fine worsted blazers, grey flannel bags and the hand-made crocodile shoes. For the country, there are the tweeds and the denims, the brogues and the penny loafers. Much of the rough wear, the plaid shirts, the bulky coats and chunky sweaters is taken from the American ranch and some from American Indian designs and patterns, mostly Navajo.

No account of Ralph Lauren is complete without mentioning the range of toiletries for men and women under the names Polo and Lauren.

The shop is a wonder in itself. It mirrors the clothes and the clothes mirror it. It is a comfortable place with a gentle atmosphere where customers can sit on sofas or in leather armchairs by an open fire; they may be offered coffee, even a glass of port. Classical music is played in the background and there are always flowers around. The staff, indistinguishable from their customers, being dressed entirely in Polo Ralph Lauren, are polite and helpful.

Polo Ralph Lauren is for those who are *it*, but also for those who aspire to *it*. Somehow, here, that is not a contradiction in terms.

OPEN Monday to Saturday 10.00 am to 6.00 pm (Thursday until 7.00 pm)

# Henry Poole

■ 15 SAVILE ROW                                        734 5985
  W1X 1AE
  (*Bespoke tailor*)

It is no accident that Henry Poole's tailor's shop has the feel of a grand London Club, for, despite the shop window, there are all the trappings of a club: the leather library chairs, the jockey scales and weights book (*circa* 1870 to the present day), the copy of *The Times* (un-ironed) and *Country Life* on the table beside a decanter (only water at the time of writing) and glasses, and, most important of all, that quiet, gentlemanly club atmosphere. Their 'membership' is large, often grand too; the 'club servants' are respectful, discreet and trusted old friends, who never forget a customer. This endemic feel is nothing new. The original Henry Poole (imortalized by Disraeli as Mr Vigo in his novel, *Endymion*), was known affectionately as 'Old Pooley' and his large premises were invaded daily by Society to 'partake of his fine Claret and Hock and to puff "Pooley's" cigars'. He was also the largest, and one of the best, tailors of his day, something that is equally true today.

About 90 per cent of Henry Poole's clients come through word of mouth (many are handed down from generation to generation), but that is not to say that the remaining 10 per cent are any the less well looked after (there was no truth in the rumour that J. Pierpoint Morgan was ever turned away by Poole's). From the moment that a customer, new or old, enters the shop, they are cosseted. They are met by either Mr Symons or Mr Cooper. The type of suit, coat, or whatever, is then discussed, and the cloth chosen.

One of the reasons that the British, and that really means the 'golden mile' around Savile Row, make the best suits in the world is that, besides their tailoring expertise built up over the centuries, they have the best cloth. Also, as these tailors buy from cloth merchants who are mostly based in Savile Row, so they can naturally buy the best cloth. Henry Poole has a choice of 4,000 of the finest British woollens; worsteds from Huddersfield, tweeds from the lowlands of Scotland, Harris and the Shetlands, flannel from the West of England with just a few tropical worsteds and mohairs from Italy.

Cloth and style chosen (there is no house style at Henry Poole, simply what the customer wants), the cutter comes and measures the customer. First-time customers are measured completely, whatever they have ordered, for future use. The cutter then cuts a paper pattern which is kept for the customer's life (Poole's have over 5,000 patterns currently). His assistant then cuts the cloth and the jacket is given to the jacket maker, the trousers to the trouser maker, and the waistcoat to the waistcoat maker. They try to have the first fitting ready in three weeks. First-time customers, or those with an awkward shape often need a second fitting while established customers' garments go straight to the completion stage.

Henry Poole began stocking ties merely as a convenience for their customers. Now, they are an entity in their own right. Here, too, is one of the few places to buy half hose.

A bespoke suit or whatever from Henry Poole falls into the category of 'not as expensive as some, but more than others'. Where it stands out is that it is absolutely right.

OPEN   Monday to Friday 9.00 am to 5.30 pm

# Prestat

■ 40 SOUTH MOLTON STREET                                     629 4838
   W1Y 1HH
   (*Special chocolates and truffles*)

With a room full of chocolate, Prestat must be a small boy's dream palace. It is not a bad place for grown-ups either, with its fine reputation for hand-made chocolates. It is a deserved reputation too, with the same consistent, high quality for the last 75 years. The original recipes are still used, and some of the chocolates are made on the premises by a small staff, some of whom have worked there for decades.

Prestat is best known for its truffles. These come in two varieties: plain truffles and truffle bombs (those covered in chocolate powder). Both types come in an exciting range of flavours: rum, champagne, brandy, coffee and orange. They can be bought in any quantity, from a single truffle to an 8lb carton –the cartons varying in size from ¼lb upwards.

Prestat chocolates also come in many shapes, sizes and flavours. The staff will mix up a box on request, either a simple carton or something more elaborate, like the Connoisseur Assortment. Inexplicably, the rose and violet creams are the most popular of the soft varieties. Other delicious goodies include coffee mints and double mints, brandy cherries ('Morello cherries marinated in pure brandy over 18 months'), and ginger. Best of all are the *marrons glacés* freshly prepared to order. Prestat also stock Turkish Delight that is sold in a wooden drum.

As if that were not enough, they make dozens of figurines, Paddington Bear being their latest addition. They have a positive menagerie of animals, mostly domestic, like dogs, cats, horses, ducks, pigs and an elephant. Chocolates tend to double as presents and at Prestat they will send their wares to any part of the world (not too hot). They have special present boxes, especially for Valentine's Day, Mother's and Father's Days; chocolate telegrams or hearts with any wording, delivered anywhere, within reason, by hand.

OPEN    Monday to Friday 9.00 am to 6.00 pm, Saturday 9.30 am to 5.30 pm

# James Purdey and Sons

■ AUDLEY HOUSE                              499 1801/2
57–58 SOUTH AUDLEY STREET        499 5292/3/4
W1Y 6ED
(*Gun-maker, shooting accessories*)

The name of Purdey has been synonymous with the very best of hand-made, sporting guns since the founding of the firm in 1814, a reputation as sound then as it is today. Theirs is a long and closely guarded reputation (the original James Purdey trained with the doyen of gun-makers, Joseph Manton, who admitted that, 'Purdey gets up the best work next to mine'). The firm thrived, buying out the bankrupt Manton's premises in Oxford Street before building their own model workshops and shop in South Audley Street, where they are today. Their success is largely due to family continuity: there were four generations of the Purdey family as owners and chairmen, and three generations of the Lawrence family as factory managers and managing directors. The present chairman, the Honourable Richard Beaumont, has a cousin, Nigel Beaumont, poised to take over on his retirement.

Equally important, if not more important, is the continuity of their workforce. Purdey's have always operated an apprentice scheme, so are constantly bringing on their highly skilled craftsmen: barrel-makers, actioners, ejector-men, stockers and engravers. They are, therefore, well set up for the foreseeable future. Each man sticks to his particular skill, and initials his own work.

Today, Purdey's reputation rests on just seventy guns a year. The road to owning a Purdey is exciting, expensive and long in that there is a delivery time of between two and two-and-a-half years for side-by-side ejector game guns, three to three-and-a-half years for an over-and-under, the mechanisms being more complicated, and three-and-a-half to four years for a rifle. First, an appointment is made with the chairman in the Long Room, and the type of shooting is discussed in detail, and in which country the gun is to be used: English guns are chambered for 2½-inch cartridges, whereas the American standard cartridges are 2¾-inches. However, the English game gun is suitable for every type of shooting in Britain. The personal preferences of the customer are discussed, like the length of the barrel, the height of the rib, the choke, the action, the lever (straight or curved), single or double triggers, left or right shoulder, and so on. The customer is measured and, with the aid of an 'electric gun' (a beam of light is 'fired' at a watercolour of a pheasant on the wall), the 'cast off' or 'cast on' is measured. The stocks are chosen from plain, rough-hewn blocks of walnut, and the type of engraving that is preferred, standard fine or Purdey extra finish. Anything can be engraved to order. Cases are extra. It is an exciting day when the gun, or pair, are handed over in the Long Room.

The Long Room is one of the most fascinating rooms in London. It doubles as the chairman's office and is a testament to the past and present excellence of Purdey's. Here are the portraits of the four generations of Purdey's and their successors, and photographs of satisfied customers (many of them from extinct, and extant, Royal houses of Europe). Here, too, are the pieces of Purdey *memorabilia*, like a pair of miniature hammer-less game guns, complete with case, no more than three inches long. It is well worth asking to see the room as the request may coincide with an indulgent moment of the chairman.

Like other top London gun-makers, Purdey's sell all makes of good quality second-hand English shotguns (mostly their own). They also repair all recognized makes of English shotguns. Purdey's have their own cartridges. Formerly, these were all filled by hand, to order, in a room in Audley House (the fillers wore felt boots so as not to make a spark), but the practice was thought too dangerous and was discontinued. These were 'bespoke' cartridges; the older the customer, the lighter the charge. Today, Purdey cartridges are loaded for customers with a standard charge.

Another side to James Purdey and Sons is their clothes, gifts and accessories. Here there is everything for the gun and for those who care about shooting (a term that neatly embraces not only men, but also those splendid women shots, and their spouses). For the gun, there are the cleaning kits, beautifully boxed in green canvas-covered cases complete with rosewood rod, snap caps and oil bottles, and Purdey's special never-rust oil. Very useful is their lambswool pull-through. Here too are the hand-made turnscrews (precision screw-drivers) in a leather case, but who would dare to remove the plate and tamper with the mechanism of a Purdey?

Behind the main shop, with its panelled walls, trophies and Royal Warrants, is the accessory shop. Here there is a cartridge bag for everyone: large ones for those big bag days, small ones for those blank days; bags (in hide) with regimental straps, tweed, even loden cloth, that doubtless double as hand-bags. Here too is one of the most complete selections of shooting clothes in London. The majority of Purdey's clothes have been designed by them, and so are just that little bit different and hence that little bit special. The Purdey jacket, made by Grenfell, has (at the time of writing) a removable alpaca lining; their waxed clothing comes in all sizes and styles, including a waxed-cotton over-skirt and a cape. Then there are the loden jackets and men's tailored shooting jackets with breeks to match, and the ubiquitous quilted jackets, but again, being Purdey's, they are extra-special (brown or olive green, patch pockets and shoulder gussets for shooting). Their knitwear is good value (and fun – *vide* the pheasant or labrador knitted sweaters).

Besides a good shooting library (including a fascinating history of Purdey's by Richard Beaumont), there are a few well-chosen gifts: the Purdey clock with shooting scenes and enamel boxes from Halcyon Days (*see* page 75), flasks and gold-plated drinking cups and the like.

The whole place has a fine, gentlemanly atmosphere about it, where the staff are expert without being intimidating. If the nearest you get to owning a Purdey is their silver money clip (a facsimile of their lock-plate, standard fine engraving), at least you have a prime example of their fine workmanship.

OPEN  Monday to Friday 9.00 am to 5.00 pm

# H. and M. Rayne

■ 15–16 OLD BOND STREET                    493 9077
W1X 3DB
(*Shoes and boutique*)

Those who admire Rayne's shop in Bond Street would defy anyone to find a prettier shop in London (those passionate about it, would say the world). If it looks like a very grand theatre set, it is because that is precisely what it is. It was designed by the late Oliver Messel, one of the most talented set-designers and interior decorators of his day, and completed in 1959. Messel joined the two shops together in a series of arches, tented alcoves and vaulted ceilings. The interior is grand (it has recently been completely redone, faithful to the original), with hand-painted ceilings of columbines by Messel himself, gold leaf, red brocade and old chintz.

In fact, the theatrical connection goes back to the founders, Henry and Mary Rayne, who specialized in shoes for actresses – satisfied customers included Lily Langtry, and later Gertrude Lawrence, Vivien Leigh and Marlene Dietrich. The continuity is still there, for Rayne still manufacture a shoe designed especially for Gertrude Lawrence.

It is really for their women's shoes and handbags that H. and M. Rayne are best known, although quite recently they have branched out from this shop into boutique and costume jewelry. Their shoes are famous (they hold two Royal Warrants to the Queen and Queen Elizabeth, the Queen Mother). Everything, including their handbags, is made in their own factory in North London to a high standard. Their style can only be described as classic, but styles that last for ever, sling-back shoes, peep-toe shoes, spectator (two-tone) shoes and the like. However, where the basic concept remains the same, this style alters marginally with fashion, like the height of the heel or the colour. These 'classics' are generally thought of for the older woman, but other styles, like their court shoes, are ageless. At the time of writing, a new collection of shoes is being designed by Bruce Oldfield (*see* page 124). Evening shoes are another Rayne speciality. There is a handbag to go with every style of shoe, day and evening.

Rayne also have other top designer shoes like those of Andrea Phister from Italy: very elaborate and ornate, but very much in the 'fun' category.

With the vogue for costume jewelry, Rayne have a collection from Monty Don (*see* page 117), based largely on Edwardian pieces. Not surprisingly, their collection of shoe-clips is best.

Exclusive to Rayne's in the Bond Street shop is the collection of boutique clothes, mostly from America. Besides the cocktail dresses (the 'little black numbers'), they specialize in what the Americans call 'hostess gowns', elegant flowing all-in-one dresses. These, designed by David Brown, come in all shapes and sizes, both for day and evening wear.

Rayne's shoes are available in other H. and M. Rayne shops and shops within shops, but the Bond Street shop is the one to visit even if you are not going to buy a pair of shoes, a handbag or whatever. But then, how do you know?

OPEN    Monday to Friday 9.00 am to 6.00 pm, Saturday 9.30 am
        to 5.00 pm

# John Rigby

■  5 KING STREET                                             734 7611
   WC2
   (*Rifle-maker, shooting accessories*)

Rigby's make rifles. Their followers agree that they are the finest rifle-makers (as far as such things can be quantified), but then they, and Rigby's, have been saying so since 1735.

Rigby's make and sell every popular calibre of rifle, and they can make any other calibre on request. At the top end of their bespoke range are the double-barrelled rifles, .416, .458 and .470 (allow between two and three years for delivery). Each Rigby rifle is hand-made, and beautifully finished. The engraving is either their own deep scroll, or anything to the customer's order, like gold inlay or a game-scene.

Most of the other Rigby rifles are built on the original Mauser actions. Again, these are all hand-built to the customer's specification and calibre, with or without telescopic sights. Again, they make in all the popular calibres, including their big game rifles, .375 and .458 and the new .416 BRNO Magnum action rifle. Especially popular is their light-weight stalking rifle. Delivery is around nine months, less if a partly finished rifle is worked on. Rigby's are less well known for making shotguns, but they do, both sidelock and boxlock. There is generally a good selection of second-hand rifles, mostly their own make.

They are now above ground in Covent Garden. It is a slip of a shop (which they share with D. Roberts), with, fortunately, no room for 'shooting accessories', other than ammunition, cartridge bags and belts. Rigby's, through their present managing director, David Marks, offer a complete service, including the repair of all rifles and shotguns. The big-game trophies around the walls are a testament to the success of their trade. Today they can, if asked, arrange a safari to go with their big-game guns.

OPEN    Monday to Friday 9.30 am to 6.00 pm

# Saint Laurent Rive Gauche

■ 113 NEW BOND STREET                                 493 1800
W1
(*French, women's boutique*)

■ 135 NEW BOND STREET                                 493 0405
W1
(*For men*)

■ 33 SLOANE STREET                              584 4993/0561
SW1
(*For men and women*)

The nomenclature of Saint Laurent Rive Gauche is simple: Yves St Laurent began his mighty empire on the Left Bank, the *rive gauche*, of the Seine, and used that name for his shops that sell women's and men's boutique clothes. While Yves Saint Laurent keeps his own couture collections exclusive to Paris, a distillation of those collections is sold through his boutiques. Being ready to wear, they are therefore comparatively cheaper. As with many of the chains of boutiques, the decor and feel of the place is standard in every shop. At Saint Laurent Rive Gauche the decor, created by Isabel Hebay, is no less attractive and smart for being dark and sombre in black and russet, with clever lighting.

Yves Saint Laurent has been creating imaginative clothes for decades. Their strength lies in that they are extremely well cut, designed to flatter the figure (or to camouflage it if necessary). His designs are right for any age. Saint Laurent clothes are also economical, in that as they last for several seasons a wardrobe can be built up a piece at a time from different collections. His use of the same fabrics keeps that continuity (there is always something in wool or cotton gabardine and flannel for winter), as does his amazing use of colour.

The same is true for Saint Laurent's men's tailoring. Here is the classic English suit, beautifully cut. His dinner jackets in a light wool are exactly right, like his pure cashmere blue blazer with its gilt YSL buttons. As with both men's and women's clothes, Saint Laurent designs 'from head to foot, day and night.'

As the late Lady Rendlesham, who set up the Saint Laurent Rive Gauche shops in London, said, 'Clothes should work for you, rather than you having to do a lot of work for the clothes.' At Saint Laurent Rive Gauche, it is the clothes that do the work.

OPEN   Monday to Saturday 9.30 am to 6.00 pm (Thursday until 7.00 pm in Bond Street, Wednesday until 7.00 pm in Sloane Street)

# John Sandoe

■  10 BLACKLANDS TERRACE                                      589 9473
   SW3 2SR
   (*Bookshop*)

This is a friendly, neighbourhood bookshop. As the friendly neighbourhood is Chelsea and the customers tend to be on the esoteric side, John Sandoe has been feeding them just the right diet of books for many years. Here, within six little rooms and four staircases is everything for the reading man and woman, their offspring too. There is nothing technical or scientific on offer, nor are there salacious paperbacks or 'good-bad' reads; just a fine selection of fiction and non-fiction works.

The table in the centre of the first room is piled high with the latest publications. Then, shelved around the book-lined walls (and stacked on book-lined floors and book-lined treads of the stairs), is the rest of the stock. John Sandoe has books that you want to read, and a good deal more that you ought to have read. He is strong on biographies and memoirs with a good selection of history. There are proper travel books and many titles on art, architecture, cooking and wine (many would shelve them together, each being a subdivision of the first). There is sport and outdoor life (that includes gardening), and indoor life that covers music and drama. Modern fiction is separate from literature and poetry; humour is in a class of its own. Children's books, largely classic, are in the basement: on the first floor are paperbacks (mostly the cheaper versions of what is on offer downstairs).

John Sandoe is more often than not in his shop. He is assisted by those who appear to have been with him forever, or look as if they are about to leave to start a book-shop on their own. Either way, they all know where everything is (being so cramped for space, no book is much more than an arm's-length away anyway). The shop has a gentle feel, almost as if it would be impolite to hurry.

OPEN   Monday to Saturday 9.30 am to 5.30 pm
       No credit cards

# The Singing Tree

■ 69 NEW KING'S ROAD                                    736 4527
  SW6
  (*Doll's house specialists*)

To visit The Singing Tree is to bite into that little cake marked 'Eat Me' in *Alice in Wonderland*, where everything is for sale, perfectly represented at one-twelfth scale. Over 250 different suppliers make up every imaginable household item for a doll's house, from the house itself down to a sewing acorn just one-eighth of an inch long (the top unscrews to reveal needles, pins and cotton reels).

Although the shop is quite small, so, of course, is the stock, which means that they can carry a huge range. There is shelf

142

upon shelf of such delights as 'Hepplewhite' four-poster beds, 'Sheraton' dining tables and sets of 'Regency' dining chairs. There are sets of wine glasses, 'Delft' dinner services and 'silver' knives and forks. They sell the occupants of the houses too, perfectly produced dolls, mostly in period dress, with porcelain faces and glass eyes. In the 'decorators' section, there are dolls-house wallpapers, printed to their own design, also Do It Yourself Kits of furniture. Nothing is missing; there are even minute *petit-point* canvases of Persian rugs and carpets. For the 'artisans', there are lighting sets that work and baths, bidets, basins and lavatories that do not. Where most of their stock is modern, they also carry a large selection of old and antique doll's-house furniture. There is generally a good selection of antique and modern doll's houses, from a grand eighteenth-century town house to a modest dwelling (like their counterparts, with prices to match). A comprehensive catalogue of what is on offer at any time is published spasmodically (£2.00 plus 50p for postage in the U.K.) for their mail-order customers, the majority of whom are overseas. Once paid for, the goods are packed by experts and sent all over the world.

Another speciality of The Singing Tree is that they can make up anything to do with a doll's house to order. Pictures can be copied, photographs reduced (in sepia only) and framed, all in about two weeks. Even favourite dogs and horses can be reproduced (preferably from a photograph) to the same one-twelfth scale.

This is a shop for connoisseurs. It has an air of a nursery invaded by the grown-ups, with the children on best behaviour. The dedicated owners, Anne Griffith and Thalia Sanders, are there every Wednesday. The staff are equally committed, with a genuine love of their subject.

OPEN   Monday to Saturday 10.00 am to 5.30 pm

# Frank Smythson

■  54 NEW BOND STREET                                    629 8558
   W1Y 0DE
   (*Leather and stationery*)

'Your tailor will be delighted to see you wearing a Smythson's diary' runs one of Smythson's advertisements. And so he should, for where most other diaries are hard and inflexible, and so upset the cut and the line of a suit, theirs are slim and supple. It was the original Frank Smythson (a printer and stationer who founded the present firm over a century ago), who first hit on the idea of making diaries with blue paper. So what? As writing does not show through blue paper as much as white, he could use thinner paper, and hence reduce the thickness of his diaries. So clever.

Today, Smythson's produce over 100 varieties of their diary in every type of leather, fabric and colour, for both pocket and desk. There are the Featherweight Diaries in pastegrain or pigskin leathers, even in such exotic skins as lizard. There are the Wafer Diaries in white lamb and crushed morocco, or finely water-marked tie-foulard silks; or the Wee-Blue Diary, just 2½ inches by 2 inches, and many more that just differ in the number of days to a page, the type of opening and the size. Desk diaries are naturally much larger, and rejoice in such wonderful names as 'The Hourly Engagements Remembrancer', 'The Cosmic' or the 'Businessman's Organiser', with the ultimate in diaries being the Premier or Royal Court, which are bound in tree-calf leather. Then there are the sporting diaries, especially the Badminton which lists every race meeting in the country and all the major sporting fixtures, such as International matches, the Waterloo Cup (coursing) and the like. Diary wallets come in the same leathers and take refills. Smythson's will initial everything. Another service that Smythson's offer is to send a new diary every year, unprompted, until asked to desist by the executors.

Diaries are obviously seasonal fare, but Smythson's do have a huge range of address and telephone books. Here are double address books divided into social and business, home and abroad, and, for chic city dwellers only, books divided into London, Paris and New York. Then there are those useful little books for recording all those useful details: golf scores, betting books, stocks and shares books, one for 'Blondes, Brunettes and Redheads' – presumably for casting directors. Smythson's are also renowned for bound record books, whether they be for recording visitors, game shot or fish caught, also hunting journals, polo journals for matches, with space for ponies played and for comment, as well as wine cellar books. Smythson's can make up anything if the standard issue does not suit but, obviously, with special printing it comes expensive. Then there are the press-cutting books and the photograph albums, in three sizes, and three colours, either half- or full-bound and two sizes of Florentine paper bindings and leather corners.

Another of Smythson's fortes are their desk accessories in leather. There is something dependable and solid about these as they have been making them for years, in exactly the same styles, colours and leathers. If something wears out or is lost, it can be replaced. Here are 15 items for the desk top, from a blotter or stationery rack to a waste-paper basket or letter rack with a lid. Again in leather are the fine wallets (some original with three pockets for pounds, French francs and dollars) and leather attaché cases.

But it is for stationery, engraving and printing that Smythson's are best known (they are, after all, By Appointment to the Queen with many clients among the *Corps Diplomatique* and the three armed services). The stationery room is downstairs, comfortably furnished in a style that is reminiscent of the writing room of a smart hotel, save for the samples of paper and engravings. Here there is just plain, old-fashioned quality – even the paper sizes are Imperial (more regal with Kings and Dukes). They have ten different papers, each milled with the Smythson watermark, including the popular Bond Street Blue.

Apart from the plain papers and envelopes, most of the stationery they sell is die-stamped to the customer's requirements, with the address, an illustration, arms, crest monogram, or whatever. The paper can be hand-bordered, that is the borders of each sheet painted a different colour, even double-bordered. The envelopes can also be hand-bordered and lined in tissue paper, and die-stamped like the paper. The copper plates for the invitation cards are all hand-engraved. There are also experts on hand to advise on etiquette. Smythson's will also print anything, like a bookplate, that is within the bounds of good taste.

A beautifully embossed invitation card that came from Smythson's, or a crisp, die-stamped letter that arrives in its matching envelope, is an equal joy to send as it is to receive, whatever the respective occasion or content. Well, almost.

OPEN    Monday to Friday 9.15 am to 5.30 pm, Saturday 9.15 am to 12.30 pm (the stationery room closes 15 minutes earlier)

# Philip Somerville

■ 11 BLENHEIM STREET                                   629 4442
W1
(*Hats*)

Philip Somerville designs and makes hats. He also happens to design and make hats extremely well, as his many distinguished clients will verify, season by season, year by year. It was not surprising, however, that his earliest collection was 'in the school of Otto Lucas' (the legendary milliner), since he was Lucas' assistant and took on four of his late pupil-master's staff when he set up on his own account.

145

Today, his style is very much his own. His hats are classic. They are elegant and chic, versatile too with each one faithful to the milliner's maxim that 'every hat should fit 50 faces'. Although not dictated to by fashion, Philip Somerville does consult the major fashion houses before working on his own collections, so his hats are at least compatible with the latest mode.

Here, there is every kind of hat. They are thoroughly 'safe' hats, right for the occasion, whether it is to launch a ship (or a daughter), to open the local fête or attend a race meeting (that said, Mr Somerville does admit to enjoying a little 'fantasy' for Ascot). His 'After 5' hats, with the glitter and the nets, are a speciality. There are just a few creations for brides and bridesmaids. He is also renowned for using only the very best fabrics. He uses the finest paribuntal and parisisal straw hats from China, to be dyed, shaped and made up by him. Trimming is another mark of his hats; note the exquisite hand-stitched satin around some of the brims, or the bows, or hat-pins, or whatever he decrees.

It is, however, for his bespoke hats that Philip Somerville is best known. He can make up any of his styles to match a particular outfit, in the same, or complementary, fabrics. These hats are made entirely by hand, by his own workforce above the salon and take about two to three weeks (allow much longer for Ascot).

The shop owes much of its decor to the hats, as indeed it should (they stand on 'trees' in no apparent order). Where bespoke customers are whisked upstairs, those who come for a hat off the 'twig', or one of those velvet berets seen on every chill race-course in the country, are ably looked after below. As every customer leaves the salon with her hat in its white, hexagonal box, autographed in black by Philip Somerville, she at least knows that, whatever else, her hat will be absolutely right.

OPEN   Monday to Friday 9.30 am to 5.30 pm

# Swaine Adeney Brigg and Sons

■ 185 PICCADILLY                                        734 4277
W1V 0HA
(*Saddlers, whip-makers, umbrellas*)

There is a sense of continuity about Swaine Adeney Brigg, for, not only have they kept the business in the firm hands of a Swaine, Brigg or, as today, an Adeney, they have occupied their

original site in Piccadilly since 1750. They began as whip-makers, branching out into walking sticks, umbrellas, and saddlery. The firm is still expanding, three centuries later, with country clothing, guns and polo equipment.

Today, there is still a demand for whips, and Swaine Adeney Brigg produce the largest selection of whips anywhere, including whips for carriage-driving, dressage, polo, racing, and four different hunting crops.

Surprisingly, there is still a huge demand for walking sticks and canes today, and Swaine Adeney produce many hundreds every week. The sticks come in all shapes, sizes, and woods. Those for the town are elegant in malacca, rosewood or some exotic wood, with a variety of handles, including ivory and silver, some with cast-silver animal heads. The ferrules are of buffalo horn, although rubber is also used for safety. Virtually any type of walking stick can be made to order. There is always a large selection of antique and old walking sticks, some with such novelties as corkscrews, watches, monoculars, or flasks in the handle. Another speciality is the Swaine Adeney sword stick (with two lengths of blade), and the stick .410 shotgun.

It is not surprising that the Brigg umbrella is world-renowned. Completely hand-made, it is smart, tough and durable, and never turns inside out. There are two types of umbrella, the 'classic' and

147

the 'traditional', which differ only in the materials used. The classic umbrellas have such exotic handles as malacca cane, ivory or leather, either lizard skin or crocodile skin. The traditional umbrellas have handles of cherrywood, whangee and ash, with a gold or silver band (solid or plated), for personal engraving. The covers are of the best English taffeta silk (peculiar only to Brigg), nylon or cotton. Like the canes, they make a sword umbrella with a hickory handle and a Wilkinson Sword blade.

Sold alongside these specialities of Swaine Adeney Brigg manufacture, is everything for the country person. Here, there is everything for the horse and rider. Their saddlery room (which includes their Swaine Adeney all-purpose Spring Tree Saddle) is complete; there is everything by way of riding clothes too, whatever the equestrian pursuit. Their country clothes are genuinely for the country; not for them some chichi urban designer's pastiche. They cater for true country living, including the green Hunter Wellingtons and the complete range of Barbours (in their own room); all practical kit that has unfortunately become classed, in some eyes, as a uniform. Here too are those essential items for the country, like the picnic baskets and tartan rugs, or just fun pieces like car mascots, with some more unusual ones like hedgehogs, frogs and golfers.

Swaine Adeney Brigg also sell guns, both modern (from that fine Birmingham gun-maker, Westley Richards), and second-hand (the better makes of English guns). The Piccadilly Gun Room in the basement has everything for the shooting man, and woman, by way of clothes, cartridges, cartridge bags, belts, boots, dog-whistles, and the like.

As saddlers, Swaine Adeney have built up a reputation for fine leatherwork, where the skills of the saddler and harness-maker have been applied to the making of attaché-cases and luggage. The luggage, in every size of case and bag, is robust, either all in leather, or in canvas with a leather trim. For the present buyer, there are the usual leather-bound photograph frames, address books and similar, together with some more imaginative things like a leather-bound opera book, a mahjong set, ivory chess sets, and Pickwick playing cards. They also have their own gift certificates.

There is exactly the right feel about this shop; the rich, red carpet and the mahogany cabinets where everything is uncluttered and nicely displayed. The walls are lined with sporting paintings, engravings and prints, from the seventeenth century to the twentieth century, all of which are for sale. The staff, some venerable, add an air of quality to the place.

OPEN   Monday to Friday 9.00 am to 5.30 pm (Thursday until 7.00 pm), Saturday 9.00 am to 5.00 pm

# Tiffany

■ 25 OLD BOND STREET                                    409 2790
W1X 3AA
(*Jewelers*)

If there was a prize for the most attractive shop in Bond Street, then it would doubtless be won by Tiffany's. It is positively enchanting. Here the windows are always original and witty, arranged for amusement rather than display (the legendary Gene Moore who does the windows in Tiffany's, New York, started them off in London for their opening in 1986). Then there is the shop itself: open, bright and welcoming, with a jaunty feel about the place; the same goes for the young staff, all of whom are patently enthusiastic about everything going on at Tiffany's.

There is something for everyone here, whether a fun present in silver or an important piece of jewelry, with price tags to match. At Tiffany's, there are the inexpensive trifles – the silver drinking straws or silver worry beads, the pretty key-ring or scent bottle. There are imaginative presents too, like the silver kaleidoscope and, something to save a marriage if your spouse squeezes the toothpaste in the middle, a silver key to roll up the tube from the bottom. Inexpensive but impressive presents, and decidedly Tiffany's, are their bridge cards and scorers.

Tiffany's have always filled a need. Here too are the silver Christening presents: toys and rattles (some that double as executive toys), Christening mugs and dressing-table sets. Also in silver is a collection of jewelry: bracelets, earrings and brooches, some plain, some with gold, but all in that bold and distinctive Tiffany style. It is typical of Tiffany to use something like silver for these pretty, but comparatively inexpensive, pieces, an area often neglected by other jewelers. Then there are those pieces in 18-carat gold, often in a complete collection with a particular theme. Typical are their twisted rings and earrings, both plain or with some adornment like diamonds set in platinum, cuff-links, or, as at the time of writing, the Kiss Collection of intertwining Xs, even the heaviest of wedding rings. There is always a diamond and gold collection of pretty, modern pieces, like stars and moons, or 'flashes of lightning'.

Practically everything that is sold here has been designed and made in their studios in New York, and is exclusive to Tiffany's (anything that has not been made by them will certainly be a 'one-off'). Their success rests with craftsmanship and design. Tradition and conservatism have come to mean old-fashioned and staid, but at Tiffany's, they believe that the best in modern and original design has evolved naturally from the past. Leading the in-house designers are Jean Schlumberger, Elsa Peretti, and, more recently, Paloma Picasso. They work exclusively for Tiffany's and their collections embrace everything, from silver and gold to creations in precious and semi-precious stones, ceramics, glass and a complete collection of watches by Paloma Picasso.

These Picasso watches, bejeweled and plain, for both men and women, are novel in design in that the numbers are represented by little balls, in silver, gold, diamonds or whatever, outside the watch-face. Tiffany's own Atlas watch (and clock) is so named after the Titan, who seemingly has given up carrying the world in favour of the clock outside their New York shop.

Where there are just a few classic pieces of jewelry, like solitaire engagement rings with the famous six-pronged 'Tiffany setting', it is what can almost be described as their hall-mark of using rare, and relatively unknown, gem stones that makes their pieces so unusual and different. There are three, little-known gem stones special to Tiffany's: Kunzite, 'gloriously lilac or orchid in colour, very hard . . .' named after their gemologist Dr Kunz; Tanzanite, 'deep blue gems with flashes of purple, green and red', and Tsavorite, 'even more brilliant and durable than an emerald'. They also use other semi-precious stones like amethyst, rubellite, citrine, tourmaline and black onyx in their creations. These gem stones are then cut and made up into an exquisite piece, or pieces, that form part of a designer collection. They are usually set in 18-carat gold, and complemented with precious stones: diamonds and pearls, for example, go particularly well with them.

Continuing the theme of using semi-precious stones with gold and silver, there is always a splendid range of inlaid jewelry, like the 'Tiffany Allures' collection of a choker, bracelet and ear-clips of gold inlaid with black onyx and mother-of-pearl. Other exciting combinations of stones are lapis lazuli, nemiatite (in beads for necklaces), citrines and tourmalines, also enamel. Their pearls, which come in various qualities (including those vast, perfectly matched ones) are unstrung, so that they can be made up with a clasp to order.

Besides this contemporary jewelry, there is always a selection of antique jewelry (Tiffany's own, of course). Also in the same genre as that designer jewelry is their glassware and ceramics. Here are such beautiful things as glass candle-sticks, burgundy and claret glasses, and, very special, are their champagne flute glasses. Alongside the dinner services, the ceramic animals and the Limoges patch boxes, are two sizes of the famous Tiffany box in porcelain, light turquoise and 'tied' in colour, with a white ribbon and bow.

Everything, from the cheapest piece to the most expensive, is wrapped, packed, and tied up in a Tiffany box. Tiffany's is very special: after all, where else could you find the largest canary diamond in the world for sale (the 'Tiffany diamond' of over 128 carats with 90 facets) and a silver pencil at a little over £10, both in the same shop?

OPEN    Monday to Friday 9.30 am to 5.30 pm, Saturday 10.00 am to 4.00 pm

# Truefitt and Hill

■ 23 OLD BOND STREET                              493 2961/8496
MAYFAIR
W1X 3DA
(*Gentlemen's hairdresser and toiletries*)

It is not surprising that Truefitt and Hill has an air of gentility about its Bond Street establishment considering their clientele. Nor is it surprising that it should have a reputation for what is now considered pre-War service, for most of the staff have worked there for over 30 years, one for 40.

A haircut at Truefitt and Hill for the first time is nothing less than a grand experience. The place is smart and comfortable, the magazines current and readable, and those who cut your hair expert. It takes time and they take trouble. Here you find all those long-forgotten touches – the cotton wool pushed around the collar, the towel to wipe the face dipped in cologne, the shoes cleaned, free of charge as all part of the service. The team of barbers, led by Mr Beard, has been joined by four women comparatively recently (that is ten years ago which, for a company nearing its 200th anniversary, is comparatively recent).

Truefitt and Hill are equally renowned for supplying the needs of their gentlemen in the bathroom. Not only do they have their own colognes, aftershave and hair oils – Trafalgar, West Indian Limes or Fresh Limes, Spanish Leather, Old English and Clubman – but also other, well-known brands like Penhaligon's (*see* page 129) and Creed from France. There are shaving soaps and shampoos, bath soaps and bath oils. They have those huge bath sponges that have become almost a memory and pure badger shaving brushes, even cut-throat razors and razor strops (not generally recommended).

OPEN    Monday to Friday 9.00 am to 5.30 pm (last orders 5.00 pm), Saturday 9.00 am to 12.30 pm (last orders 12.00 noon)

# Geo. F. Trumper

■ 9 CURZON STREET                                              499 1850/2932
  W1Y 7FL
  (*Gentlemen's hairdresser and toiletries*)

■ 20 JERMYN STREET                                            734 1370
  SW1

There is a definite atmosphere of Edwardian London about Geo. F. Trumper, gentleman's perfumer and hairdresser's shop in Curzon Street. That feel is created through a combination of the decor (the polished mahogany booths, with marble surrounds to the basins and the scuffed-leather chairs, the generous mahogany counter piled with bottles and the glass-fronted cabinets) and the friendly, yet deferential service.

Although there is a certain severity about a standard Trumper's haircut, the customer can, of course, have his hair cut exactly as he wishes. But Trumper's are equally famous, if not more famous, for what Osbert Sitwell described in his autobiography as their 'secret preparations, lotions and balms with names like those of nymphs, Floureka, Eucris, and others'. While Floureka and Eucris are still going strong, the 'others' run into dozens of different fragrances.

The nomenclature of the Trumper Collection of colognes and aftershaves evokes a sense of martial grandeur (Marlborough and Wellington), of importance (Curzon and Astor), or just of the country (Wild Fern). Other aftershaves and colognes bear such famous names as Eau de Portugal, Extract of Limes, Spanish Leather and Bay Rum.

Then there are those Sitwell favourites in Trumper's hairdressing preparations, Floureka and Eucris, the famous Isis, Fernil and, among many others, Coronis, created to mark the Coronation of King George VI. Like some of their special preparations of shampoos and conditioners, most of these 'secret preparations' come in attractive bottles with their distinctive crown tops. Also attractively presented are their shaving soaps (violet, rose and almond) in turned, cedar wood bowls, or in an Edwardian ceramic pot. These soaps come in various fragrances including one called Goats Milk.

Special is their whole range of shaving kits – badger brushes and razors of every size. Here too are their accessories, complete manicure sets, seven sizes of natural sponge (including an elephant ear sponge), and their own bone combs and toothbrushes. What more could any gentleman's bathroom ever need?

OPEN   Monday to Friday 9.00 am to 5.30 pm, Saturday 9.00 am to 1.00 pm

# Turnbull and Asser

■ 71/72 JERMYN STREET                                    930 0502
SW1Y 6PF
(*Men's and women's shirts, and haberdashers*)

This is a proper shop. What is more, it has always been a proper shop, and true to its origins as a haberdashery. It has always had a reputation of being that little bit different, that little bit more special; just as it has always been patronized by those who want something a little different and a little bit more special too. From the beginning, they have been sartorial innovators: it was they who put the clocks on men's socks in the Twenties; they who introduced the floral and kipper ties, the mark of the Sixties, and the shirts that would make even the technicolor Jacob blanch in the Seventies. These ideas were undeniably eccentric, but all done with such panache and conviction that they are acceptable. Turnbull and Asser have made a name for themselves world-wide, and they make certain that they live up to it. After all, if it is from Turnbull and Asser it must be all right.

Over the years, they have built up an especial relationship with the mills that supply their exclusive shirting material. This means there is always something new and exciting on offer, whether a particular stripe or a funny check, a certain shade or an amusing pattern. The basement (lower ground floor in estate agent's parlance) is given over entirely to shirts. It is called the Churchill Room after one of their more famous customers, Sir Winston (they made his green velvet siren suits, one of which hangs in a display cupboard here). The choice of shirts seems limitless, with everything in every size (the sleeves are purposely long so they can be shortened if required). Here, there is every type of shirt to reflect character or profession, from the unadventurous to the outspoken. Here too are shirts in every type of fabric – the silks and the cottons, the voiles and the like. Their evening shirts are special.

The bespoke shirts are in the neighbouring shop in Bury Street where there is the same huge choice of fabrics and styles. New customers, however, need to take at least six shirts for the first order. Turnbull and Asser will then make up the chosen one first to ensure it is right before completing the order. Allow at least two months for delivery. Embroidered initials, coronets or whatever are extra. Here too are the ready-to-wear suits, including those in such exotica as cashmere; special are their dinner jackets and the frogged velvet smoking jackets. Handsome are their own raincoats.

As haberdashers, Turnbull and Asser sell everything associated with their trade. Here are the ties, like Jane, both bold and plain. Shirt fabrics are made up into pyjamas and the like; similarly the tie material finds its way into everything, particularly dressing gowns (at the time of writing, they are into marvellous, heavy, hand-blocked silks in several colourways). Here too are the braces and the leather gloves, the handkerchiefs and the socks, in several weights and even more colours. There are also sweaters in every hue and yarn, from the flimsiest lamb's wool to 8-ply cashmere and knitted silk.

The shop itself has the air of a rather jolly London club but there are no hushed whispers here. It has the appearance of a London club too, with its plush red carpet and panelled walls – note the foxes' masks wearing bow ties. The resemblance to a club goes further still, with the customers more like members, and the staff like club waiters (all presumably called Charles, whatever their baptismal name). If you are not looking for something a little bit special, do not bother with Turnbull and Asser (after all, there are plenty of places to go to for that); if you are, then you will be surely satisfied here.

OPEN  Monday to Friday 9.00 am to 5.30 pm, Saturday 9.00 am to 4.00 pm

Next door is Turnbull and Asser's ladies' shop which also bears their unmistakable stamp, mostly in the form of blouses and shirts. Shirts and dressing gowns are made up in their shirting or tie fabrics. The shop could be called James Drew (*see* page 42), (they do, after all, sell the same clothes), but the name of Turnbull and Asser seems to have the greater ring.

154

# Valentino

■ 160 NEW BOND STREET                          629 3181/
  W1                                                        493 2698
  (*Designer boutique for women and men*)

■ 173–174 SLOANE STREET                        235 5855/0719
  SW1

A glance is enough for the *cognoscenti* to recognize anything designed by Valentino, for that same unmistakable chic and glamour are there, be it an evening dress, a man's tweed jacket, a piece of furniture, a fabric, even an Alpha Romeo (in London, delete the furniture, fabric and the Alpha). For the non-*cognoscenti*, Valentino is renowned the world over for his beautiful clothes: the big, squared shoulders, the narrow waist, the slightly shorter skirts and the flash of red are the give-away clues to his collections (his clients are almost as recognizable as his clothes). His clothes are refined and beautifully tailored. The fabrics are always interesting: apart from the straight-forward wools and cashmeres, silks and chiffons, furs, leathers and suedes and the rest of the natural fibres, there are other interesting twists, like the appliqués – velvet on suede, or suede on the softest leather for blousons and skirts.

Valentino Boutique is exclusive. Of Valentino's evening dresses and ball gowns, there will be only one or two in any one shop (it also lowers the odds of that dreaded confrontation of another wearing the same dress). Obviously, his collections of day dresses and suits, coats and skirts cannot be equally exclusive. His clothes and accessories are colourful and fun: here are gloves covered with sequins and marcasites, the odd piece of jewelry, bright scarves and the like. Another important part of the all-embracing Valentino service is his scent, Valentino by Valentino, a unique mixture of fruit and flowers.

A diffusion of the Boutique collection is called 'Miss V', with its younger look and less expensive price tags. The collections appear when they are most needed. The pre-winter is the precursor of the Boutique collection, while the cruise collection (for that winter sun) is a taste for summer.

The basement is given over mostly to men. Here are the classic, tailored suits, both Boutique and the slightly less expensive L'Uomo. These, too, are in interesting fabrics (such as the suits in pure silk) and beautifully cut to the Valentino style. There are also unusual overcoats; typical is one in a dark herringbone with an astrakhan collar. Valentino achieves what sounds improbable, like mixing two different but matching tweeds in one jacket (the sleeves, collar and back in a broad check, the front in a herringbone). Sweaters are a speciality, with different knits (cable, ruched or just plain) to accentuate pattern and colour. Very special is the hand-knitted double-breasted waistcoat in 3-ply cashmere. More on the casual side are the Valentino jeans, blousons and shirts.

The shop has a marble-hall-look about it – sparse but none the less the right foil for the Valentino collections. The staff are predictably chic and patently proud of what they are selling. With Valentino, their customers are patently proud of what they are wearing.

OPEN    Monday to Friday 10.00 am to 6.00 pm, Saturday 10.30 am to 6.00 pm

# Wartski of Llandudno

■ 14 GRAFTON STREET                                    493 1141
 W1X 3LA
 (*Antique jewelry, Fabergé*)

As dealers in antique jewelry (and so technically outside the scope of this book), it is well worth making an exception for Wartski of Llandudno, specialists in the works of Carl Fabergé, the Russian Court jeweler. They have been buying his works since 1925, when the Soviets began selling off the treasures of the State Antiquariat. Since then, Wartski's have had seven Fabergé Imperial Easter eggs, as well as the Tsarina's tiara. Today, they have around 150 pieces of Fabergé at any one time, with a good representation of his work. Obviously their collection varies, but there is always an interesting selection of Fabergé animals (as collected by HM The Queen and others most Royal). There are also exquisite flowers in crystal vases, clocks and watches, also indispensable Fabergé items like electric bell-pushes, cigarette cases, snuff-boxes, picture frames, paper knives and parasol handles. Add to that the pieces of jewelry, from a small brooch to possibly a tiara, and here is one of the finest collected works of the great master.

Wartski's welcome anyone interested in Fabergé to their shop, and are delighted to show off the pieces on display, along with other non-Fabergé pieces, like an eighteenth-century gold snuff-box. The present chairman, Kenneth Snowman (grandson of the founder, Morris Wartski from Llandudno), is the world authority and a prolific writer on both Fabergé and eighteenth-century gold boxes. Those who are really keen can even buy a video on the subject.

156

Besides these exotic pieces, Wartski are also noted for nineteenth-century revivalist jewelry, English silver, icons and Russian porcelain (an acquired taste, but much collected).

The shop has just the right feel about it; not too imposing yet grand enough with Louis XVI sofas and Sheraton chairs. The staff of seven are all knowledgeable and are equally helpful whether making a mega-purchase or just browsing – after all, a stunning piece of Fabergé is only half the price of a production motor car.

OPEN   Monday to Saturday 9.00 am to 5.30 pm

## The Watch Gallery

■ 129 FULHAM ROAD                                          581 3239
   SW3 6RT
   (*Watches*)

Lord Cut Glass, with his 'kitchen full of time' from Dylan Thomas's *Under Milk Wood*, would be very much at home in The Watch Gallery, for there they claim they have 'All the Time in the World for You'. Yet despite the preciseness and accuracy of the stock, there is a timeless quality about the place. From the moment you pass through the door, an out-sized, outside edge of a Viennese watch with a light and chrome bar that 'still stands' at 12 o'clock, and enter their showrooms (shop seems a somewhat inadequate term for the Lou Engerhausen designed interior of yellow and black), you enter a capsule of time.

Elegantly draped around the room are the staff, each member a veritable horological genius, personally instructed by the makers of each of the watches on sale. The watches themselves are draped in glass cases and cabinets, each display having its own theme – oyster and pearls to show off an antique Rolex Oyster; an art deco desert island, complete with waving palm, for a waterproof number and so on. The same precise atmosphere pervades downstairs where there is a birds-eye maple bar, stools, a sofa and some comfortable chairs, where all of their clientele are offered anything from champagne to lime Perrier water, even expresso coffee. Here the same un-pressured approach continues.

The choice of watches is wide, comprehensive and designed for all tastes, and pockets, and wrists. Most of the top names are here, from Audemars Piquet and Baume and Mercier to Klok Watches and Hippipotime; from Hubolt, Ulysse Nardin and Jaeger-LeCoultre to Fortis, G of Time and Momo (who also make Formula 1 steering wheels). They also have tray upon tray of antique watches, the likes of Patek Philippe, Cartier (*see* page 28), Asprey (*see* page 11), Vacheron et Constantin and Rolex. Some come with their original certificates and boxes. If they do not have a particular watch in stock (either in London or their showroom in Bath) for a client, they pride themselves on being able to find it. Often a watch will not 'go' for a client and they will exchange it as many times as is necessary. Their own team of watch repairers are not proud and will work on any watch whether it is from The Watch Gallery or not.

Poor Lord Cut Glass, what jealousy: tick tock, tick tock . . .

OPEN  Monday to Friday 10.30 am to 7.00 pm, Saturday 11.00 am to 6.00 pm


# Watches of Switzerland

■ 16 NEW BOND STREET                    493 5916/6339
W1Y 9PF
(*Swiss watches and clocks*)

If you want to know the time, ask a policeman. If you want to know the time to a tenth of a second, go to Watches of

Switzerland's New Bond Street showroom where you will find a Patek Philippe master clock on the wall. Here, amid a rather faded grandeur somewhat reminiscent of a Sixties hotel with red, patterned carpet, distressed and gilded white walls and chandeliers, you can find some of the finest watches produced in the world. As their name implies, Watches of Switzerland trade in Swiss watches but, as they are quick to point out, they deal in quality first which allows a few non-Swiss horologists to be represented as well.

Watches of Switzerland pride themselves on service, not only for the initial sale, but for the life of the watch, which could be for many generations. On entry to the shop you are assigned a *vendeur/vendeuse*, well-trained and horologically experienced, and then shown to a desk. There your preference (and 'pocket') are delicately explored, then trays of watches are brought to suit both.

All the very best names in watches are represented here, those companies tried and tested over decades, some even centuries. Their watches have often timed the Olympic Games (Omega); been chosen by Tchaikovsky, Wagner and Einstein, even Queen Victoria for Prince Albert (Patek Philippe); been up Everest (with Lord Hunt) and on the deepest sea dive (Rolex Oyster), and worn by Neil Armstrong to time his first steps on the Moon (Omega, again). Add to this list some of the other top names: Tissot, Rotary, Seafarer ('reasonably priced, water-protected watches, tough, accurate and reliable' they claim), Jean Renet (their own in-house brand) and the famous Longines, Bueche-Girod, Baume and Mercier, Vacheron et Constantin, Ebel, Piaget and Blancpain, *Horologers dès 1735* to complete their range. They also stock the better clocks, including an intriguing atmospheric clock.

After-sale service of Watches of Switzerland is also efficient. They recommend that their watches be overhauled every two to two-and-a-half years; this service takes anything between four and eight weeks, depending on the season. Not unreasonably, they service only the makes they stock and preferably nothing over 25 years old. Straps and batteries for quartz watches can be changed while you wait. They value watches for insurance purposes (£3 plus 1 per cent) and will engrave, inexpensively, security markings of your post- or zip-code on the back of the watch.

As they claim at Watches of Switzerland, there is plenty of time to choose.

OPEN    Monday to Saturday 9.00 am to 5.30 pm

# The White House

■ 51–52 NEW BOND STREET                    629 3521
  W1Y 0BY
  (*Linen, lingerie and childrens' clothes*)

The very name of The White House conjures up a variety of feelings for all past customers. For some, they are childhood memories of being dragged there by nanny for clothes (the 'Fairy Corner' with its domed ceiling with moon and stars, and plaster characters is now gone with the latest improvements); to others, it has always been a place to buy the best in linens, or special nightwear and clothes of a certain style: those who remember it as a hand laundry are out of luck because that has closed down.

The White House began as a linen shop, and three generations later, it is still selling quality linen. Here is the largest selection of bed linen, often with matching towels. Here are the sheets in crisp Irish linen, percale, Egyptian cotton or cotton voile, in every size from a small, child's bed to king-size. Special to them (in London) are the linens from D. Porthault of Paris. Here too is a fine selection of bed-covers: they also make up any bed-cover to order – they were not remotely phased when one client asked for one in mink, large double-bed size.

There is the same wide choice with the table linen, especially the fine linen damask table cloths and napkins (they are in the *Guinness Book of Records* for the largest, single table cloth ever woven, measuring 200 metres in length, and for supplying 1,500 napkins incorporating a royal insignia). Other less mighty table-cloths are those of plain linen with Deruta embroidery. For finer work, there are the hand-embroidered linen and organdie table cloths and place settings with both appliqué-work and embroidery. The linen table sets are also exquisitely worked in a variety of styles (one in gold thread), in linen or linen/organdie. There are also attractive breakfast sets by D. Porthault with matching breakfast china. Here, as in every department, the White House will accept commissions.

From the original Irish-linen handkerchief counter has grown a whole men's accessory department. Here they stock Paisley silk dressing gowns and such luxuries as cashmere and nylon socks, silk socks and Swiss cotton or silk pyjamas. Shop here also for silk, and Swiss cotton underwear from Zimmerli, and the whole Smedley range. The handkerchiefs are still there, both for men and women, in Swiss cotton with the same rolled-edges and wide variety of decoration, including hand-embroidered initials.

The ladies' fashion is thoroughly 'safe'. Here there are suits and dresses for day and evening wear that would grace any formal occasion. There is a host of carefully chosen accessories, sweaters, bags, scarves, gloves and belts. Cruisewear is another White House speciality.

The White House, however, are more adventurous with their nightwear, which is all made in their own workrooms to their own designs. Top of the range are the very pretty pure silk satin negligée sets and the silk satin nightgowns. There are many other nightgowns in cotton voile, cotton polyester and pure wool, while the dressing gowns come in a similar variety and combination of fabric, from pure silk satin with quilted cuffs to satin-bound acrylic and cotton towelling. Silk pyjamas, slips, camisoles and suspender belts complete this extensive range.

The same mark of conservatism and tradition runs through the children's department. Here, there is everything for the new-born baby to children up to the age of twelve. For the new-born baby to have everything, there is a reproduction Victorian metal swinging cradle trimmed with ecru Nottingham lace with everything, but everything, to match (including a nursery bin and coat hangers). For the Christening, there is a selection of lace robes. After that, the clothes are for every age: The White house is particularly strong on party wear, especially girls' 'designer' party dresses. Many of the styles have lasted for generations: the hand-tailored tweed coat with velvet collar, the barathea sailor coats, or the hand-smocked wool suits and buster suits. There is also a children's tailoring service.

There is no bustle here; there are no cash tills, money just disappears up old-fashioned tubes. The *vendeuses* keep a sense of continuity about the place. Some span two generations, which all helps to reinforce the memory.

OPEN   Monday to Friday 9.00 am to 5.30 pm, Saturday 9.00 am to 1.00 pm

# Zandra Rhodes

■ 14a GRAFTON STREET                                              499 6695
W1
(*Women's fashions, especially evening dresses*)

As a designer, Zandra Rhodes is unique. She has earned herself the position of one of the foremost, and influential, designers in England today with an international reputation. Her clothes, particularly her evening dresses for which she is so famous, are all *nonpareil*. She describes her dresses as works of art (examples are to be found in the Victoria and Albert Museum), and, being so individual, they are timeless. Zandra Rhodes is never afraid to express herself, even to the point of shocking – she once created a collection that was partially inspired by a dress by Schiaparelli of the 1930s. However, her work is generally less reactionary.

Zandra Rhodes began as a textile designer. When the dress designers fought shy of her bold fabrics, she began to cut round her patterns to form the shape of the dress or garment. Her designs are often based on her travels, or from something that catches her eye in a museum or gallery. Among the dozens of 'designer-venues', there has been a Spanish collection, a Japanese collection, one based on Ayers Rock in Australia, a zebra from Kenya, an Aztec collection from Mexico, and, at the time of writing, 'Secrets from the Nile'. Other collections have been inspired by objects as diverse as banana leaves, feathers from the Museum of the American Indian, or a painting by Fragonard.

An evening dress from Zandra Rhodes has been created, from start to finish, entirely in-house. As her designs are screen printed, mostly on chiffon, by her own printers, she can use different colourways to make each dress virtually exclusive. The dresses are cut and made up in her own workrooms, entirely by hand. Crinolines, that double as wedding dresses or evening dresses, are also special to Zandra Rhodes.

In addition to her collections, Zandra Rhodes takes special orders. She designs many wedding dresses, sometimes designing for the whole bride's family – the bridesmaids, the mother of the bride, even the invitations.

There is always something new and exciting from Zandra Rhodes (at the time of writing, she has a collection of jewelled denim). Her day wear, Zandra Rhodes II, of skirts, dresses, trousers and suits, and Zandra Rhodes Knitwear, is less expensive than her evening wear but still has her distinctive look. There is also a collection of accessories, handbags and stoles (some beaded like her sweatshirts), and Zandra Rhodes pantihose and socks.

The shop itself is a fine extension of the Zandra Rhodes theme; entirely pink with a tented ceiling, it is dominated by a surrealist tree above pink cushions.

When you buy a dress here, you are given a silk square which is printed 'This is one of my special dresses. I think it is an artwork that you will treasure forever. Everything made by me is an heirloom for tomorrow'. It probably is.

OPEN    Monday to Friday 9.30 am to 6.00 pm, Saturday 9.30 am to 5.00 pm

162

# Glossary

*Argyle*: diamond pattern on sweaters and socks.

*bespoke*: made exclusively to the customer's order, as opposed to ready-made.

*bird's-eye*: lightly flecked, spotted pattern on cloth, socks, etc.

*couture*: design and making of high-quality, fashionable clothes.

*covert coat*: man's light greenish/brown short coat, often with velvet collar, for town and country wear.

*Fair Isle*: distinctive geometric pattern and colours from the Fair Isle, one of the Shetland Islands noted for its knitting designs in coloured wools.

*high jewelry*: really important pieces of jewelry, in design, setting and stones.

*Loden*: felt-like cloth, mostly in dull green but also blue and grey.

*nutria*: the fur or skin of the coypu, an aquatic rodent from South America.

*Paisley*: pattern of distinctive, curved, abstract figures.

*pantihose*: ladies' tights.

*percale*: closely woven, cotton fabric.

*plus-fours*: long wide knickerbockers (so named because, to produce the overhang, the length is normally increased by four inches).

*polychrome*: multi-coloured.

# Geographical Index

## BOND STREET

Bond Street, made up of Old Bond Street with New Bond Street above, and the streets that lead off it, is at the very metacentre of the smartest shopping area in London. Although unremarkable architecturally, it has always been fashionable; in the early eighteenth century it was the place to promenade, and be seen. Today, the character of the street is still very much the same, with many of those eighteenth- and nineteenth-century names still above their original premises, some even with their workrooms above.

With Old and New Bond Street, the numbering starts at the south-east corner and continues anti-clockwise around the street.

### ■ OLD BOND STREET

**H. and M. Rayne**
15–16 Old Bond Street,
W1X 3DB
493 9077
*Shoes and boutique: see page 138*

**Truefitt and Hill**
23 Old Bond Street, W1X 3DA
493 2961/8496
*Gentlemen's hairdresser and toiletries: see page 151*

**Tiffany**
25 Old Bond Street, W1X 3AA
409 2790
*Jewelers: see page 149*

**Loewe**
25a Old Bond Street, W1X 3AA
493 3914
*Spanish leather work, especially clothes and luggage*

**Chanel Boutique**
26 Old Bond Street, W1
493 5040/5171/5270
*Scent and boutique: see page 30*

**Gucci**
27 Old Bond Street, W1X 3AA
629 2716
*Shoes and leather, presents: see page 72*

**W. Bill**
28 Old Bond Street, W1X 3AB
629 2554/9565
*Lambswool and cashmere sweaters*

**Holmes (Jewelers)**
29 Old Bond Street, W1X 3AB
493 1396
*Antique silver and Sheffield plate*

164

**Agnew's Galleries**
43 Old Bond Street, W1 4BA
629 6176/9
*Fine art*

■ NEW BOND STREET

**Etienne Aigner**
6 New Bond Street, W1Y 0AR
491 7764
*Leather accessories, luggage and classic clothes: see page 46*

**Watches of Switzerland**
16 New Bond Street, W1Y 9PF
493 5916/6339
*Swiss watches and clocks: see page 158*

**Basile**
21 New Bond Street, W1
493 3618
*Italian boutique: see page 15*

**Fogal**
36 New Bond Street, W1
493 0900
*Stockings: see page 55*

**Mallett**
40 New Bond Street, W1Y 0BS
499 7411
*Fine furniture*

**The White House**
51–52 New Bond Street, W1Y 0BY
629 3521
*Linen, lingerie and children's clothes: see page 160*

**Ciro Pearls**
48 Old Bond Street, W1
493 5529
*Imitation and cultured pearls specialists*

**Frank Smythson**
54 New Bond Street, W1Y 0DE
629 8558
*Leather and stationery: see page 143*

**Frederick Fox**
87–91 New Bond Street, W1Y 9LA
629 5706
*Women's hats: see page 59*

**Saint Laurent Rive Gauche**
113 New Bond Street, W1
493 1800
*French, women's boutique: see page 140*

**Giorgio Armani**
123 New Bond Street, W1
499 7545
*Italian designer, women and men: see page 67*

**Saint Laurent Rive Gauche**
135 New Bond Street, W1
493 0405
*French, men's boutique: see page 140*

**S. J. Phillips**
139 New Bond Street, W1A 3DL
639 6261
*Antique silver, fine jewels, miniatures, snuff boxes*

**Polo Ralph Lauren**
143 New Bond Street, W1Y
9FD
491 4967
*American designer clothes for
women and men: see page
131*

**Partridge**
144 New Bond Street, W1
629 0834
*Dealers in fine art and
furniture*

**Wildenstein**
147 New Bond Street, W1
629 6861
*Dealers in fine art*

**Louis Vuittron**
149 New Bond Street, W1Y
9FE
409 0155
*Luggage*

**Kilkenny**
150 New Bond Street, W1Y
0DH
493 5455
*Everything Irish, especially
Waterford crystal*

**Hermès**
155 New Bond Street, W1Y
9PA
499 8856
*Leather, women's and men's
fashions: see page 91*

**Valentino**
160 New Bond Street, W1
629 3181/493 2698
*Designer boutique for women
and men: see page 155*

**Asprey**
165–169 New Bond Street,
W1Y 0AR
493 6767
*Jewelry and leatherwork,
particularly luggage,
presents: see page 11*

**Birger Christensen
(incorporating Maxwell
Croft)**
170 New Bond Street, W1Y
9PB
629 2211
*Furrier: see page 21*

**Karl Lagerfeld**
173 New Bond Street, W1
493 6277
*Women's designer fashions:
see page 106*

**Cartier**
175 New Bond Street, W1Y
0QA
493 6962
*Jewelry, including watches:
see page 28*

■ THE ROYAL ARCADE West of Old Bond Street.

**Charbonnel et Walker**
One The Royal Arcade
28 Old Bond Street, W1X
4BT
629 4396
*Chocolates: see page 32*

**Grimaldi**
Twelve The Royal Arcade
Old Bond Street, W1
493 3953
*Antique pocket and wrist
watches*

■ BURLINGTON GARDENS/BURLINGTON ARCADE

The Arcade runs parallel to Old Bond Street between Burlington Gardens and Piccadilly.

Burlington Arcade was built in 1819 by Lord George Cavendish, and is carefully preserved in its original Regency style. The banning of 'hurrying, whistling and singing' is strictly imposed by a uniformed beadle. The shop numbers start from the south-west corner and continue clockwise.

### Wetherall
1/2 Burlington Arcade, W1
493 5938
*Woollen reversible coats and capes*

### James Drew
3 Burlington Arcade, W1
493 0714/9194
*Women's shirts, skirts, coats and dresses: see page 42*

### Charles Clements
4/5 Burlington Arcade, W1
493 3923
*Hair brushes*

### S. Fisher
22–23 and 32–33 Burlington Arcade, W1
493 4180/6221
*Cashmere sweaters, waistcoats: see page 52*

### The Pen Shop
27 Burlington Arcade, W1
493 9021
*All types of pens: see page 128*

### The Irish Linen Company
35–36 Burlington Arcade, W1V 9AD
493 8949
*All linen: see page 102*

### N. Peal
37–38 and 54 Burlington Arcade, W1V 9AE
493 5378/9220
*All cashmere, women and men: see page 127*

### Penhaligon's
55 Burlington Arcade, W1
629 1416
*Fragrances, soaps: see page 129*

### Lord's
66–70 Burlington Arcade, W1
493 5808
*Cashmeres, shirts, ties, scarves*

■ GRAFTON STREET West of New Bond Street.

### The Medici Gallery
7 Grafton Street, W1
629 5675
*Art publishers, cards*

### Wartski of Llandudno
14 Grafton Street, W1X 3LA
493 1141
*Antique jewelry, Fabergé: see page 156*

### Zandra Rhodes
14a Grafton Street, W1
499 6695
*Women's fashions, evening
dresses: see page 162*


■ BRUTON STREET West of New Bond Street.

### Holland and Holland
33 Bruton Street, W1X 8JS
499 4411
*Gun-maker, all shooting ac-
cessories, presents: see page
98*


■ BROOK STREET East and West of New Bond Street.

### Halcyon Days
14 Brook Street, W1Y 1AA
629 8811
*Enamel boxes, antiques and
clocks: see page 75*

### Courtenay House
22–24 Brook Street, W1
629 0542
*Country clothes and lingerie:
see page 38*

### Penhaligon's
20a Brook Street, W1
493 0002
*Fragrances and all toiletries:
see page 129*

### Roland Klein
26 Brook Street, W1Y 1AE
629 8760
*All women's designer clothes*


■ SOUTH MOLTON STREET A pedestrian walkway between
Brook Street and Oxford Street.

### Butler and Wilson
20 South Molton Street, W1
409 2955
*Costume jewelry: see page 26*

### Prestat
40 South Molton Street, W1Y
1HH
629 4838
*Special chocolates and
truffles: see page 134*

### Browns
23–27 South Molton Street,
W1
491 7833
*The cream of an international
fashion emporium: see page
22*

168

■ BLENHEIM STREET West of New Bond Street.

**Philip Somerville**
11 Blenheim Street, W1
629 4442
*Hats: see page 145*


■ ST CHRISTOPHER'S PLACE

This is a pedestrian walkway, attractively laid out, but notoriously hard to find from crowded Oxford Street. The narrow entrance is just east of James Street that borders Selfridges.

**The Mulberry Company**
11–12 Gees Court
St Christopher's Place, W1
493 2546
*Leatherwork, especially suitcases, country clothes: see page 118*


■ PICCADILLY

Numbering starts at the north-east corner and continues anti-clockwise.

**Cordings**
19 Piccadilly, W1
734 0830/0868
*All foul-weather kit and all men's clothes: see page 36*

**Fortnum and Mason**
181 Piccadilly, W1A 1ER
734 8040
*Department store, provisions, wine: see page 56*

**Swaine Adeney Brigg and Sons**
185 Piccadilly, W1V 0HA
734 4277
*Saddlers, whip-makers, umbrellas: see page 146*

**Hatchards**
187 Piccadilly, W1V 9DA
437 3924 or 439 9921
*Booksellers: see page 85*

### ■ CURZON STREET

Curzon Street runs parallel to Piccadilly between Park Lane and Berkeley Square.

**Geo. F. Trumper**
9 Curzon Street, W1Y 7FL
499 1850/2932
*Gentlemen's hairdresser and toiletries: see page 152*

**Heywood Hill**
10 Curzon Street, W1Y 7FJ
629 0647
*Superior booksellers, old and new books: see page 93*

### ■ SOUTH AUDLEY STREET

South Audley Street, with its attractive buildings, runs parallel to Park Lane.

**Thomas Goode and Company**
19 South Audley Street, W1Y 6BN
499 2823/4291
*China, glass and silver: see page 68*

**Hobbs**
29 South Audley Street, W1
409 1058
*Exciting provisions: see page 99*

**James Purdey and Sons**
Audley House
57–58 South Audley Street, W1Y 6ED
499 1801/2 and 499 5292/3/4
*Gun-maker, shooting accessories: see page 135*

### ■ MOUNT STREET

Mount Street runs between Berkeley Square and South Audley Street.

**John Baily and Sons**
116 Mount Street, W1
499 1833
*Poulterers, game dealers and butchers: see page 14*

170

■ DOVER STREET Off Piccadilly, running north to Grafton Street.

## Crolla
35 Dover Street, W1
629 5931
Avant-garde *men's fashions:*
*see page 40*

■ ST JAMES'S STREET

This is one of the prettiest streets, and the heartland of the London clubs. It runs south from Piccadilly towards St James's Palace and Pall Mall. Starting from the south-east corner, the numbers continue anti-clockwise.

### Berry Bros and Rudd
3 St James's Street, SW1A
1EG
930 1888/5331
Export: 930 5631
*Wine merchant: see page 19*

### James Lock
6 St James's Street, SW1A
1EF
930 5849/8874
*Hatter: see page 110*

### J. Lobb
9 St James's Street, SW1A
1EF
930 3664/3665
*Bespoke boot- and
shoe-maker: see page 109*

### Robert Lewis
19 St James's Street, SW1A
1ES
930 3787
*Cigar merchant: see page 106*

### Davidoff of London
35 St James's Street, SW1
930 3079/1361/5887
*Cigar merchant*

### Kent and Curwen
39 St James's Street, SW1
409 1955
*Special sportswear, cricket
sweaters, colours*

### Justerini and Brooks
61 St James's Street, SW1
493 8721
Export: 486 7272
*Wine merchant*

### William Evans
67a St James's Street, SW1A
1PH
493 0415
*Gun-maker, shooting
accessories: see page 47*

■ PICCADILLY ARCADE The Arcade runs south from Piccadilly to Jermyn Street.

**Budd**
1a/3 Piccadilly Arcade, SW1
493 0139
*Pyjamas and ties*

**Sarah Jones**
12 Piccadilly Arcade, SW1
499 8415
*Pretty, modern silver*

■ DUKE STREET

**Alfred Dunhill**
30 Duke Street,
St James's, SW1Y 6DL
499 9566
*Pipes, tobacco, men's
fashions, watches, luggage:
see page 43*

**H. R. Higgins (Coffee-man)**
79 Duke Street, W1M 6AS
629 3913/491 8819
*Coffee: see page 95*

**Green's Champagne and
Oyster bar**
36 Duke Street
St James's, SW1
930 4566
*Champagne bar, wine
merchant: see page 71*

■ JERMYN STREET

Another attractive street, Jermyn Street runs parallel to Piccadilly
and leads into St James's Street.

**Bates the Hatter**
21a Jermyn Street, SW1
734 2722
*A wonderfully chaotic shop,
selling hats of every
description*

**New and Lingwood**
53 Jermyn Street, SW1Y 6LX
493 9621
*Shirts and shoes, ready-to-
wear and bespoke: see page
121*

**Geo. F. Trumper**
20 Jermyn Street, SW1
734 1370
*Gentlemen's hairdresser and
toiletries: see page 152*

**Turnbull and Asser**
71/72 Jermyn Street, SW1Y
6PF
930 0502
*Men's and women's shirts,
and haberdashers: see page
153*

**J. Floris**
89 Jermyn Street, SW1Y 6JH
930 2885
*Fragrances and soap: see
page 53*

**Paxton and Whitfield**
93 Jermyn Street, SW1Y 6JE
930 0250/0259/9892
*Cheese: see page 126*

■ BURY STREET

**Paul Longmire**
12 Bury Street
St James's, SW1
930 8720
*Jewelry, especially cuff-links:
see page 112*

■ PALL MALL

**C. Farlow and Company**
5 Pall Mall, SW1Y 5NP
839 2423
*Fishing tackle and country
clothes: see page 50*

**Hardy Brothers**
61 Pall Mall, SW1Y 5HZ
839 5515
*Fishing rods, reels and
accessories: see page 79*

■ LOWER GROSVENOR PLACE Lower Grosvenor Place runs
between near the east end of the King's Road and Buckingham
Palace Road.

**J. A. Allen**
1 Lower Grosvenor Place,
Buckingham Palace Road,
SW1W 0EL
828 8855 or 834 5606
*Horse books: see page 9*

■ HAYMARKET The Haymarket runs between Pall Mall and
Piccadilly Circus.

**Burberrys**
18 Haymarket, SW1Y 4DQ
930 3343
*Rainwear specialists: see page
24*

## ■ PICCADILLY CIRCUS

**Lillywhites**
Piccadilly Circus, SW1Y 4QF
930 3181
*All sportswear and equipment*

## ■ SAVILE ROW

Savile Row is world famous as the home of tailoring. It runs parallel to New Bond Street, and its numbers continue anti-clockwise from the south-east corner.

**Bernard Weatherill**
8 Savile Row, W1Z 1AF
734 6905
*Bespoke tailors, especially hunting clothes*

**Kilgour, French and Stanbury**
8 Savile Row, W1
734 6905/3906
*Bespoke tailor*

**H. Huntsman and Sons**
11 Savile Row, W1X 2PS
734 7441
*Bespoke tailor: see page 100*

**Henry Maxwell**
11 Savile Row, W1X 2PS
734 9714
*Boot- and shoe-makers: see page 115*

**Hardy Amies**
14 Savile Row, W1
734 2436
*Couture dress designer: see page 78*

**Henry Poole**
15 Savile Row, W1X 1AE
734 5985
*Bespoke tailor: see page 133*

**Tommy Nutter**
18-19 Savile Row, W1
734 0831
*Stylish bespoke tailor: see page 123*

**Bowring, Arundel and Company**
31 Savile Row, W1X 1AG
629 8745
*Shirtmakers, hosiers and tie-makers*

■ CLIFFORD STREET Leading into Savile Row from Bond Street.

**W. and H. Gidden**
15d Clifford Street, W1X 1RF
734 2788
*Saddlers, and all riding wear:*
*see page 65*

**J. Dege and Sons**
16 Clifford Street, W1X 2HS
734 2248
*Bespoke tailors, especially*
*country tweeds, sporting and*
*military colours*

■ OLD BURLINGTON STREET Between Clifford Street and Burlington Gardens.

**Wig Creations**
12 Old Burlington Street,
W1X 2PX
734 7381/3
*Wig makers*

**Herbert Johnson**
13 Old Burlington Street,
W1X 1LA
439 7397
*Men's and women's hatters*

■ REGENT STREET

Regent Street runs between Piccadilly Circus and Oxford Street. Although it does not have quite the *cachet* of Bond Street, there are still a few luxury shops, mostly larger stores.

**Aquascutum**
100 Regent Street, W1A 2AQ
734 6090
*Rainwear and traditional*
*clothes: see page 10*

**Hamleys**
188–196 Regent Street, W1R
6BT
734 3161
*Every conceivable children's*
*toy*

**Garrard**
112 Regent Street, W1A 2JJ
734 7020
*Jewelers: see page 60*

**Liberty**
210–220 Regent Street, W1
734 1234
*Home of the famous Liberty*
*print and Far Eastern wares*

**Burberrys**
165 Regent Street, W1R 8AS
734 4060
*Rainwear and clothes: see*
*page 24*

■ SOHO

Soho, nestling behind Regent Street and Shaftesbury Avenue, is sadly best known as 'the centre of the red light' in London. However, there are still a few specialist shops (mostly food shops) that are worth a visit.

■ BREWER STREET Tucked in off Regent Street going east.

**Richards**
11 Brewer Street, W1
437 1358
*Traditional fresh fish and shell-fish*

**Just Games**
62 Brewer Street, W1R 3PN
437 0761
*Every kind of board game, including gambling equipment*

■ OLD COMPTON STREET

**I Camisa**
61 Old Compton Street, W1
437 4686
*A real taste of Italy*

**Patisserie Valerie**
44 Old Compton Street, W1
437 3466
*Fresh cakes and bread*

■ COVENT GARDEN

Covent Garden is dominated by the large covered market that used to be London's fruit, flower and vegetable market. Today, it is a collection of shops and stalls. Around lunchtime, there are usually performances from 'street entertainers'.

■ NEW ROW

**Naturally British**
13 New Row, WC2N 4LF
240 0551
*Hand-made crafts, country clothes and presents: see page 120*

■ FLORAL STREET

**Paul Smith**
43–44 Floral Street
Covent Garden, WC2E 9DJ
379 7133
*Men's designer clothes: see*
*page 125*


■ KING STREET

**John Rigby**
5 King Street, WC2
734 7611
*Rifle-maker, and shooting*
*accessories: see page 139*


■ WELLINGTON STREET

**Penhaligon's**
41 Wellington Street, WC2E
7BN
836 2150
*Fragrances and all toiletries:*
*see page 129*


■ KNIGHTSBRIDGE Knightsbridge is another important luxury shopping area. Although still with its share of luxury shops, it has an entirely different feel from Bond Street and the surrounding streets, possibly as it is more residential.

**Harvey Nichols**
Knightsbridge, SW1X 1RJ
235 5000
*Exclusive fashion, furniture*
*and furnishings: see page 83*

■ BROMPTON ARCADE

A row of shops beside Knightsbridge Underground Station.

**The Italian Paper Shop**
11 Brompton Arcade, SW3
589 1668
*Marbled paper and desk
accessories: see page 103*

Opposite, behind the
triangular patch of grass:
**Cutler and Gross**
16 Knightsbridge Green,
SW1X 7QL
581 2250
*Ophthalmic opticians, and
sunglasses: see page 41*

■ BROMPTON ROAD

**The Scotch House**
2 Brompton Road, SW1
581 2151
*Highland dress and tartans*

**Fogal**
51 Brompton Road, SW3
225 0472
*Stockings: see page 55*

**Charles Jourdan**
39–43 Brompton Road, SW3
581 3333
*Shoes and boutique: see page
33*

**Harrods**
Knightsbridge, SW1Z 7YX
730 1234
*Largest department store in
Europe: see page 81*

■ BEAUCHAMP PLACE

Beauchamp Place is a short street that runs between the
Brompton Road and Walton Street. There are some fine shops
here but, unfortunately, the street always appears rather scruffy
as there is usually some building work going on somewhere, and
the area is often littered with skips and builder's rubbish. The
street numbers run anti-clockwise from the north-east end.

**Kanga**
8 Beauchamp Place, SW3
581 1185/589 3784/225
1611
*Specialized dresses: see page
105*

**Caroline Charles**
11 Beauchamp Place, SW3
589 5850
*Women's designer fashions:
see page 27*

**Bruce Oldfield**
27 Beauchamp Place, SW3
1NJ
584 1363
*Women's designer fashions:*
*see page 124*

**The Beauchamp Place Shop**
55 Beauchamp Place, SW3
589 4118/4155
*Good British women's*
*designer fashions: see page 16*

**Jasper Conran**
37 Beauchamp Place, SW3
589 4243
*Women's and men's designer*
*fashions: see page 104*

**Monty Don**
58 Beauchamp Place, SW3
1NZ
584 3034
*Costume jewelry: see page*
*117*

■ WALTON STREET

To the west of Beauchamp Place is Walton Street, part
residential, part shopping. The shops are narrow and pretty, with
art galleries, interior decorators, 'present' shops, and the like.

**Tapisserie**
52 Walton Street, SW3
581 2715
*Tapestries, canvasses and*
*wool*

**John Boyd**
91 Walton Street, SW3
589 7601
*Milliner*

8

■ SLOANE STREET

Sloane Street runs between Knightsbridge and Sloane Square.

**Browns**
6c Sloane Street, SW1
493 4232
*Fashion emporium: see page*
*22*

**Saint Laurent Rive Gauche**
33 Sloane Street, SW1
584 4993/0561
*French, women's and men's*
*boutique: see page 140*

**Chanel Boutique**
31 Sloane Street, SW1
235 6631
*Scent and boutique: see page*
*30*

**The General Trading**
**Company**
144 Sloane Street
Sloane Square, SW1X 9BL
730 0411
*China, glass, leather, toys,*
*furnishings, presents: see*
*page 62*

**Valentino**
173–174 Sloane Street, SW1
235 5855/0719
*Designer boutique: see page
155*

**Courtenay House**
188 Sloane Street, SW1
235 5601
*Country clothes and lingerie:
see page 38*

■ PAVILION ROAD

Pavilion Road is a narrow, cobbled street running parallel to
Sloane Street.

**Bellville Sassoon**
73 Pavilion Road, SW1
235 3087/5801
*Fashion house: see page 18*

■ MOTCOMB STREET To the east of Sloane Street.

**Cosmetics à la Carte**
16 Motcomb Street, SW1X
8LB
235 0596
*Bespoke make-up: see page
37*

■ WEST HALKIN STREET Parallel to Motcomb Street.

**Eximious**
10 West Halkin Street, SW1
627 2888
*Monogrammed items and
presents: see page 48*

**William Thuillier**
10a West Halkin Street, SW1
235 3543
*Dealer in fine art*

**Cooper and Perkins**
10a West Halkin Street, SW1
245 6111
*Interior decorators*

## ■ THE KING'S ROAD

The King's Road, together with the New King's Road, stretches from Victoria to Putney Bridge. West of Sloane Square, the majority of the shops are at the lower end of the fashion market, but with a few notable exceptions. To the east of Sloane Square:

**The London Espadrille Centre**
79 King's Road, SW3
351 4634
*Every type and colour of espadrille*

**Green and Stone**
259 King's Road, SW3
352 0837/6521
*Artists' materials*

**Edina Ronay**
141 King's Road, SW3
352 1085
*Designer hand-knit sweaters: see page 46*

## ■ THE NEW KING'S ROAD

**David Linley**
1 New King's Road, SW6 4SB
736 6886
*Bespoke furniture: see page 107*

**The Singing Tree**
69 New King's Road, SW6
736 4527
*Doll's house specialists: see page 142*

**Hackett**
65a, b and c New King's Road, SW6
731 2790
*Complete gentleman's wardrobe, new and second-hand: see page 74*

## ■ ELIZABETH STREET

Elizabeth Street runs between the King's Road and Buckingham Palace Road.

**Mostly Smoked**
47 Elizabeth Street, SW1
730 8367/8368
*Smoked food: see page 117*

■ SYMONS STREET

Parallel to the King's Road, and to the west of Sloane Square (behind Peter Jones).

**Beaudesert**
8 Symons Street, SW3
730 5102
*Four-poster bed
manufacturers: see page 17*

■ BLACKLANDS TERRACE

On the north side of the King's Road.

**John Sandoe**
10 Blacklands Terrace, SW3
2SR
589 9473
*Bookshop: see page 141*

■ SYDNEY STREET

**The Chelsea Design
Company**
65 Sydney Street, SW3 6PX
352 4626
*Women's designer fashions:
see page 34*

■ OLD CHURCH STREET

To the south of the King's Road, by the Cannon Cinema.

**Manolo Blahnik**
49–51 Old Church Street,
SW3 5BS
352 8622/3863
*Italian hand-made shoes: see
page 114*

## ■ THE FULHAM ROAD

The Fulham Road runs parallel to the King's Road, to the west of Brompton Road.

**The Constant Sale Shop**
56 Fulham Road, SW3
589 1458
*Sale designer fashions*

**Butler and Wilson**
189 Fulham Road, SW3
352 3045
*Costume Jewelry: see page 26*

**The Watch Gallery**
129 Fulham Road, SW3 6RT
581 3239
*Watches: see page 157*

## ■ POND PLACE A slip of a street.

**Anouska Hempel**
2 Pond Place, SW3
589 4191
*Women's designer clothes: see page 87*

## ■ STANHOPE MEWS

Off Stanhope Gardens, and running parallel with the Gloucester Road, is Stanhope Mews West in South Kensington.

**Victor Edelstein**
3–4 Stanhope Mews West,
SW7
244 7481/2
*Women's designer clothes:
see page 45*

## ■ PARK WALK

To the south of the Fulham Road, west of Beaufort Street (and the Cannon Cinema).

**Perfect Glass**
5 Park Walk, SW10
351 5342
*'Everyday', 'Better', 'Perfect'
and 'Antique' glass of every
description*

## ■ THE CITY

There are a few specialist shops in the City (mostly for those last-minute presents), and some wine and cigar merchants.

## ■ THE ROYAL EXCHANGE

**Hermès**
3 Royal Exchange, EC3
626 7794
*Leather, women's and men's fashions: see page 91*

**Halcyon Days**
4 Royal Exchange, EC3
626 1120
*Enamel boxes, antiques and clocks: see page 75*

**Green's**
34 Royal Exchange, EC3V 3LP
236 7077
*Seriously good wine merchant: see page 71*

# Index